*The meals created from Todd's cookbook are satisfying,
both to my doctors and to me. Yum, yum, yum, yum.*

Ram Dass

*Todd cooks with conscious joy and harmony.
I heartily recommend Todd and Jia's cookbook,* Vegan Inspiration.

Kathlyn Hendricks, co-author with Gay Hendricks, *Spirit Centered Relationships*
and *Conscious Loving,* www.hendricksinstitute.com

*Todd's food is truly a gift from heaven. The recipes are lovingly created
with consciousness and healing intent. When I taste Todd's creations,
I feel the love and blessings.*

Namaste, Deva Premal, Performing artist with Miten of The Yoga of Mantra,
www.mitendevapremal.com

*As a Universal Peace and vegetarian activist, I really appreciate
Todd Dacey's practical book of nourishing Vegan recipes.
It is wonderful, also, that he includes essential educational material on
nutrition, preparing foods, and how to eat in a balanced, healthy way.
After witnessing terrible cruelty to animals at a slaughterhouse,
I could never eat meat again. As a Buddhist monk, I began to research
the words of Lord Buddha and found that there were several teachings
in which he said we should not kill or cause killing any sentient being and
not eat meat. As a result of this activism, my vegetarian campaign has led to
many people around the world, especially Buddhist monasteries and
nunneries, becoming vegetarian. I hope, with the help of this book, many more
people will overcome from causing the killing of animals and live healthier.*

Geshe Thupten Phelgye, a simple Buddhist monk following H.H. the Dalai Lama,
Member of Parliament of the Tibetan Government-in-Exile, founder of the Universal
Compassion Movement, and Universal Peace and vegetarian activist.
www.universalcompassion.org

Dedicated to my lifelong Love, Hawai'i Nei.

Infrared Photo by: Kathy Carr www.Kathleencarr.com

Pu'uhonua O Honaunau

Ho'okahi No Ka 'Aina a Me Na Kanaka
The land and the people are one. - *KAHEA Motto*

Rainbow Fusion Cuisine for Body, Mind and Spirit

Vegan Inspiration

Whole Food Recipes for Life

by

Vegan Chef Todd Dacey
with Jia Patton

BLUE DOLPHIN PUBLISHING

> *It does take effort to question whether our conventional ways
> of thinking and acting truly serve us. It takes effort to ask whether our
> lives are in alignment with the prayers and deeper purposes of our hearts.
> It takes effort to consciously make choices that deviate from the cultural
> norms, yet bring us closer to our wholeness and true health.*
>
> John Robbins, *The Food Revolution*

Published by Blue Dolphin Publishing, Inc.
P.O. Box 8, Nevada City, CA 95959
Orders: 1-800-643-0765 • Web: www.bluedolphinpublishing.com

All art and photographs copyrighted by the artists.
Cover art © Jean K Love and Francene Hart - www.francenehart.com
Cover graphic art © Cheryl Leigh Gama - www.forevervisions.com

ISBN: 978-1-57733-216-9
First printing, February 2008

Library of Congress Cataloging-in-Publication Data

Dacey, Todd.
  Vegan inspiration : whole food recipes for life / by Todd Dacey with Jia Patton.
       p. cm. — (Rainbow fusion cuisine for body, mind and spirit)
  Includes bibliographical references.
  ISBN 978-1-57733-216-9 (wire-o pbk. : alk. paper)
 1. Vegan cookery. I. Patton, Jia. II. Title.

  TX837.D145 2007
  641.5'636—dc22

                                                                        2007034453

Printed in Canada by Transcontinental Printing
 10   9   8   7   6   5   4   3   2   1

Eo mai e Haloa, Haloanakalaukapalili
Malama ia ka pokii o Haloanaka
O ka heiau iho no, he kino ko ke kanaka
O ka ai, o ka aina, o ke Akua iho no
O ka ai, o ka aina, o ke Akua iho no
O ka ai, o ka aina, o ke Akua iho no
E Ola

We rejoice the taro being the first born—Haloa the fluttery leaf
Second indeed is the people found in Haloanaka—
cared for by the food of the land
The soul lives within the body/temple of the people
For the people, the land, and the Higher Power
For the people, the land, and the Higher Power
For the people, the land, and the Higher Power
Let it live on forever!

Mahalo Nui e Todd, blessings indeed upon you and your work

Kumu Keala, Nä Wai Iwi Ola

Table of Contents

Recipes

~ Beverages ~

> *How can we change a world in which decisions that affect our health and the health of the planet for generations to come are taken in order to present economic growth at the next shareholders meeting? What can we do as individuals in this world of giant corporation greed, human and animal suffering, and environmental destruction? Each decision we make—what we choose to buy, choose to eat—will have an impact on the environment, on animal welfare, and importantly, on human health.*
>
> Jane Goodall, *Harvest for Hope, A Guide to Mindful Eating*

~ Salads ~

~ Dressings ~

~ Condiments ~

~ Dips ~

~ Sauces ~

~Soups ~

~ *Vegetables* ~

~*Main Courses*~

> *We have been through the Agricultural and Industrial Revolutions and are now in the midst of a great Environmental Revolution.*
>
> www.Joannamacy.net

~ Desserts ~

~ Cookies ~

~ Muffins & Breads ~

~ Puddings & Crisps ~

~ Cakes ~

~ Dessert Sauces ~

~ Pies ~

When you gather enough berries, you can bake the pie. Grace

Acknowledgments

I acknowledge and thank the health pioneers, teachers, and chefs whose commitment to health has given us the understandings and products available today.

I thank Jia Patton for her friendship, for the excellent meals we've enjoyed, and for the gift of all she has added by co-authoring this book

I acknowledge all the good work provided to us by so many truly dedicated and caring individuals in the medical profession. Despite the many obvious faults of the current medical system—such as profit-based policies and lack of comprehension of illness prevention—we thank the untold many who really do care and help so much.

To Grace, my most angelic light friend, thank you so much for walking this Earth embodying true Divine Love, for being there with your wide open heart with me in the heights and in the valleys, and for truly embodying Grace.

I thank my father, Joseph, for his ongoing faith in me and for his support in helping to make the dream of this book possible. You are a continuing inspiration to me.

My deepest gratitude to all my teachers, including Diamond and River of the Total Integration Institute, for being such skillful role models for true opening and for writing the Foreword for this book that says it all. Mahalo Anandi Ma, and the dolphins and whales for teaching unity so well. Many thanks to Marianna for her service and dedication which brought to fruition the first edition of this book.

Also, awesome appreciation to Mona, Grace, Erin and Isabel and all the other catering partners and fellow chefs who have helped perfect these recipes and bring cooking with love to new levels of purity and sweetness.

Much gratitude to my beloved friend and superb artist, Francene Hart, for all the wonderful artwork and support she has contributed to this project.

Likewise to Cheryl Leigh Gama whose sweet willingness to help, creativity as an artist, and skillful Photoshop skills made the cover a beautiful work of art.

Thank you Jean Love for the Mango Heaven painting on the cover and for your joyful being. From the moment I first saw your artwork it felt like home to me.

My deepest appreciation to all the members of our community for their contributions and the truthfulness, love, playfulness, and spiritual growth that we share.

And to my son, Chris, for his Divine timing to visit from New Zealand and give so much invaluable support by being an awesome son, helping me cater, and to finish this book—may the world be a home for you and all our children to thrive in peace.

Blessings and Aloha, Vegan Chef Todd

 # Foreword

Conscious Evolution. Now.

We have arrived at an extraordinarily pivotal point. There are severe breakdowns occurring at every level of life on Earth. We see these as an old context dying, the cultural media expressing the death cries of an old, outmoded domain of existence whose time is completing. Yet there are also seemingly limitless breakthroughs occurring simultaneously all over our planet. It is a new time on Earth—and rapid consciousness, evolution is a new possibility.

We are integral shamans and guides to people from many races, cultures, ages and income levels, and this is what we know: A contextual Shift is occurring <u>now</u>. If we are to move with this extraordinary opportunity, we must take responsibility to serve the evolution of ourselves and the world at the highest level possible, now. This means <u>being</u> the resolution through full embodiment of our awakened, authentic selves. This requires releasing the old context from every aspect of our lives, Beings and choices. It also entails immersing ourselves in integral life practices that support the awakening and transformation of our essential selves, our relationships and our world.

Meditation is an essential practice, but we cannot meditate our shadow away. We need to address and embrace all aspects of Being in the way they need to be responded to, if we are to be fully effective. The Emotional Body needs safety, vibration, movement, and its messages to be understood and responded to, if we are to develop into mature, responsible, emotionally intelligent human Beings. Our Hearts need our support in opening and flowering in a safe space created by us as Spirit. We need to be learning about healthy boundaries and functional empowering relationships, not only to other humans, but to all life.

Our minds need quiet, meditation, rest and illumination, and also, stimulation by being stretched and exercised through learning new things, expanding into the unknown, and original, inspired thinking. We need to make empowered integral choices such as the commitment to unconditional self-love, healing our abandonment and toxic shame, and practicing sobriety and impeccability in all that we do and contribute to our world.

As we commit to awakening and integration, we will become increasingly present in each moment and present in our Bodies. Our Bodies are as sacred as any other aspect of Being, one with all of manifestation, "God's Body." When we live in our God Body, we know we are not separate and we honor all of Life as sacred and one. We begin to feel ourselves one with Source and that we are co-dreaming our World into Being. Our lifestyle and food choices support us in waking up in the dream and being conscious of who and what we are.

We need to eat for consciousness, for vitality, and for strength, with total gratitude and humility for the food we are so bountifully supplied. It is time to heal addictive, compulsive choices so our neurology can be free, in alignment with what is true, what is love, and what is beautiful. As we purify and strengthen our Bodies, they will reveal to us the knowledge of the Kosmos through every cell that truly is created in the image of God.

Thank you, Todd, for loving and nurturing everyone you feed and showing us through your book how to continue to do it for ourselves. Ever since Todd left a delectable pumpkin and seaweed soup (now evolved to the Thai Curry, p. 143) on the stove for us when we arrived on a rainy cold day, in 1989, on the south island of New Zealand, we've known without a doubt his food was healthy, delicious, and imbued with vitality. He's made many beautiful meals for us and our students over the years, and we are so glad others will now be able to benefit from his knowledge (and recipes!).

In Peace, Beauty and Optimum Health,

Breathing....

Diamond and River Jameson

Founders of the Total Integration Institute

www.totalintegrationinstitute.com

 # Todd's Introduction

My dedication to the "healing journey" really began in the late 1980s when I was introduced to the profound principles of Total Integration. I still remember clearly the life-changing moment when Diamond Jameson, one of the facilitators at the Total Integration Institute, said to me, "How do you expect to have peace and happiness when you are eating pain and suffering?"—a principle I later came to know as Ahimsa in yogic tradition.

Thus my journey started as I began to unravel from my past—part of which was growing up on Oahu where the family business was one of the largest suppliers of animal-based foods to restaurants and hotels. This new path of living freedom integrated a vegan whole food diet for health and energy reasons. It taught how to take responsibility, release addictions and limiting beliefs, and free the nervous system from contraction by surrendering to being in the unknown and letting go of control.

While learning to navigate skillfully in new territory, I soon realized I was fascinated with exploring holistic practices and this new healthy eating style. As one thing led to another, I soon ventured into my first catering job at a workshop held at an intentional community in New Zealand where the principles of Total Integration were being shared.

As these workshops became popular and my catering became more refined, my love of preparing and serving nurturing vegan delights to spiritually focused groups grew. Through my personal continuation of the diet and Integral practices, I noticed my quality of life increasing with more joy, well being, happiness and energy. This led me to an ongoing awakening and deepening with different teachers, ministers and swamis and an unfolding of catering opportunities in Hawaii, California and Europe.

My trademark is to focus primarily on organic foods and healthy cooking with love. I have integrated lessons and information learned through my own major health challenges, working with many other wonderful, talented chefs, and ongoing explorations of spirituality and holistic health. In 1995, I was an executive distributor with a company that was on the forefront of bringing colon health information to wide popularity. Many of the people involved were on the cutting edge of the health and wellness fields, and I learned even more about the subtleties of creating optimum health and the major importance of a good diet and a clean, strong, regular digestive system.

Later, I received much experience in the practices of Karma Yoga (service) and Bhakti Yoga (devotion) as a spiritual path through working with a variety of tastes in the large retreats of a spiritual ministry. My responsibilities and education included organizing and overseeing the food preparation for two-week retreats, with up to eighty participants. Having so many varying food tastes to please, creating a spiritual environment while in the kitchen, and limited time to prepare meals helped me strive to find a diet style that was pleasing for most people, could be prepared efficiently, with love, and was still healthy.

I have learned that, as people differ in their personalities, so do they differ in response to food. Different diets work for different body types and at different times. I would hesitate to say that everyone should immediately become pure vegan, though that would without a doubt have miraculous results. I would say, though, that we have reached "point crisis" on Earth and that it makes a difference to shift to an organic diet, which involves greater awareness of the energy involved in what we eat, and making healthy choices.

To have a greater awareness level of potential hazards and make informed decisions about one's health and the health of our planet is to participate in solutions to our Earth's crises. Amidst so much worldly delusion, to be sensitive to our own life choices is tantamount. As the great mystic, Andrew Harvey, says in his book, *The Way of the Mystic:*

"It is where we are, it is what is happening. Anyone not in a trance of denial knows it. This samsara (ignorance and illusion) is highly organized, versatile and sophisticated: it assaults us from every angle with its propaganda, and creates an almost impregnable environment of addiction around us."

Purifying the body opens the door to the purification of inner tensions, contradictions, conflicts and pressures. This allows the possibility of more clarity, freedom of choice and availability to be inspired and guided to do what makes a difference. A period of cleansing and lighter wholesome foods is often valuable and necessary to skillfully and mindfully discern choices that reorient oneself to being more in integrity with ourselves and all life.

We as a society have become out-of-tune with our true nature, as diverse traumas have compromised our natural connection to all that is, and lessened our ability to feel cared for and safe. Only a society so polarized could knowingly poison the Earth, torture animals, and recklessly destroy its air. To allow an economy to be controlled by corporate greed rather than one based upon improving the quality of health for all its people is sheer folly. It becomes blatantly obvious that Divine intervention and the incarnation of many Holy beings has saved us from our misguided selves so far.

Food can be used as a tonic to help us return to the true nature of our authentic self. The Rainbow Fusion section in this book elaborates on ways to make food the most nutritious, delicious, and full of loving energy. What we eat is our most direct interface with nature as we ingest the end products of the interaction of Mother Nature's elements.

Food, like all matter, is vibrational energy. When we consume it, the vibration of the food is transferred to us. The more fresh and alive food is, the more of that energy we receive. What we put into our bodies has a direct influence on our health and consciousness. To choose cruelty-free, light, health-promoting, simple meals, prepared with love and caring, is an important part of the solution.

These healthy food choices are often the first step to a greater ability to tune into life's great mystery and to experience the profound revealing of who we are as individual cells interconnected within the universal body of creation. It is crucial at this time to become aware of the true nature and divinity of ourselves, of creation, of others, and to the authentic joy of knowing everything has purpose. Living by the Eternal Truth "to do unto others as we would have them do unto us," expressed by all great masters, is ever so important.

For many years, I have had the good fortune to commune with dolphins in the wild and have directly experienced a reference point for the unity within nature that is intrinsic to the universal principles expressed by many indigenous cultures, traditions, and teachers. This book is intended on the deepest level to be an inspiration of support in our journey to reveal our innermost essence that connects us with all other beings, to rediscover our Divine design and the beautiful part we play in making our future alive with endless possibilities.

At this time of ever increasing evolutionary unfolding, the flagrant inadequacies of the current medical system, widespread spiritual bankruptcy, and devastating environmental situations, a wave of humanity is being drawn to seek alternative ways of living. I remember well the words Dr. Terry Shintani spoke to me once, "It's like there are just a few of us swimming in the ocean trying to turn the course of a giant aircraft carrier headed for destruction." I offer *Vegan Inspiration* as a heartfelt plea for sanity as well as a compilation of the most pertinent information and practices that we have found of real value and practical application as viable alternatives to the standard American diet (SAD) and lifestyle choices.

When exploring food and recipes, we have several basic considerations. First, is it easy to prepare and will the food taste delicious? Will it leave a person feeling happily nourished,

while supporting peace and the health of the Earth as well as the person? These recipes are the result of many years of those inquiries.

There are many basic recipes that can be simply and easily modified to create exciting, delicious and healthful variations, as well as more exotic recipes that will tantalize even the most jaded vegan palate. The area of raw and dehydrated foods has been thoroughly covered by so many highly knowledgeable authors that it is not the total focus of this book, yet there are many delicious raw recipes included to give a broad foundation for this style of eating. For many, raw foods eventually become the highest choice for those dedicated to vibrant health.

After the publication of an earlier edition of *Vegan Inspiration,* I saw areas that would greatly benefit from a revision, and Jia Patton agreed to co-author and add her deliciously excellent recipes, extensive experience and cooking knowledge. What a wonderful gift!

We extend an invitation to each of you to taste the delights and receive the benefits of *Vegan Inspiration,* and to savor any ingredients that resonate with your unique being.

Please read through the book first, before trying the recipes, especially the glossary of definitions and terms. There is a wealth of pertinent information throughout the book to support the creation of beautiful meals.

Aloha and Maluhia (Peace)
Vegan Chef Todd (www.Veganinspiration.com)

> *There is a call for a new life for each of us, a life that is infused with a deeper understanding of our own being as well as a unity with all beings everywhere. Recognize that yearning and build your relationships and choices based on that.*
>
> Mata Vanessa Stone, www.AmalaFoundation.org

Todd's Prayer

This prayer is for all those worldwide who are embracing the vision and directing their lives towards helping the fruition of a new dream and reality for our Mother Earth and all beings.

That humanity might awaken to the unity of all life, our true highest purpose, living in peace and loving and caring for our fellow humans, living beings and planet.

That our food choices might embrace the potential of peace on Earth, an end to war, where armies are Peace Corps trained to save lives and care for the environment.

Where love, rather than greed, is at the forefront of purpose and the imaginable joy of having an end to poverty, so harmony in all our relations is manifest.

Where the fulfillment of life originates from the spiritual awakening within each heart rather than through the amassing of fortune and material gain.

Where religions respect one another and recognize the inherent unity, wisdom and love that is universal to all true spiritual endeavors.

To each individual who takes a step away from samsara (illusion) towards purifying in body and spirit, that will support the Divine transformation of our world.

May much grace be with you on our journey home.
In gratitude and peace, Vegan Chef Todd, "Vegananda"

The human race needs and yearns for the "Left Hand of God." It longs to be part of a world in which kindness, generosity, non-violence, humility, inner and outer peace, love, and wonder at the grandeur of creation stand at the center of our political and economic systems and become the major realities of our daily life experience.

Rabbi Michael Lerner, *The Left Hand of God...*

Jia's Introduction

Hi, I am Jia and I have contributed many of the recipes for this beautiful book Todd has so generously shared with me. I taught a vegan cooking school for fourteen years. I am the author of *Celebrate Life! From the Heart of My Kitchen to Yours* and the recipe author of *May All Be Fed, Diet for a New World* written by John Robbins. John is a wonderful spokesperson for the factory farm animals and has changed many people's lives through his writings, lectures and by his example. Where John and others have done a great job of educating so many people about the devastating truth of modern animal factory farming and the nutritional benefits of a vegan diet, I share my gift of how to prepare delicious, nutritious vegan fare.

My journey as a vegan started in 1986 when I met my yoga teacher and spiritual guide, Kali Ray (Kaliji), founder of TriYoga®. Through her example, I opted for a diet based on plant foods. This diet is known as "vegan" and is based on the yoga principle of Ahimsa, meaning to be as harmless as possible.

The Ahimsa Principle is not passive but meant to be a positive guide for meeting the challenges of daily life. It is not always obvious which of our actions are doing harm. For example, when one buys cheese that is beautifully wrapped from their local market, what are they really buying? We know an animal has not been killed for this product, so why would it not be in alignment with Ahimsa? A closer look tells us a story of cruelty, abuse and disease. This is the life our factory farm animals must endure for their entire life. The story goes beyond the animals to our precious planet herself. Modern animal factory farming is causing major devastation of our Earth. It gets down to, what is good for you and for me is also what is good for our Earth and all living beings. We have to look beyond the cheese to see how it was brought into creation. That is how deep we must look in order to follow the Ahimsa Principal. The vegan diet, when approached consciously, does the least amount of harm to our bodies, to our Earth or to other living beings.

As I looked deeper into the vegan diet and lifestyle, I found the important key was approaching it consciously. Just choosing vegan was not enough, as I wanted a diet that would support my health into my later years as well as support the health of our precious planet, and at the same time would be in alignment with my yoga principals. For my vegan diet to do all this, I turned to organically grown, whole and high vibration plant foods, from local sources except for some imported foods from sustainable, fair trade farms around the world.

What I began to see was that my joy—that is, my job or gift—was to share my knowledge about food, where to buy it, and how to prepare it in delicious, nutritious, beautiful ways. Being a junk-food vegan is not healthy and I knew people needed help making the transition to a vegan diet. A healthy vegan diet is made up of whole plant foods like fresh fruits, vegetables, whole grains, beans, nuts, seeds, sea vegetables and some *High Vibration Foods* (see page 25).

My joy of cooking has taken me on a "magic carpet ride" that I could never have imagined. My first classes started out in my home with six students. Before I could think, a local vegan live foods restaurant invited me to teach at their facility. Then I remodeled my kitchen and turned my home into a cooking school. Quickly word got out about my vegan creations and I was asked to prepare the menus and coordinate the food preparation for many large conferences including the Unity in Yoga conference at Murrieta Hot Springs for about four hundred participants and the Woman of Vision Conference at Georgetown University in Washington, DC with over five hundred participants for five days. My teaching expanded and I taught classes with more than sixty students. Through my work at the Esalen Institute, eight years in all, on the Big Sur coast of California, I met the owner of Rancho la Puerta in Mexico and was invited to be a guest chef. I have also been the guest chef at the Hippocrates Health Institute in Florida where I won their Green Cuisine Award for my Nori Lotus Flowers which was made with the Sunny Almond Spread on page 89.

Through my writing and teaching I show others how to build nutrition and flavor into their dishes as well as how to develop color and an artful presentation. Flavors are built by specific cooking techniques, having fresh organic ingredients, and by using fresh herbs and spices. An important aspect of making food is serving it. An artful presentation takes just a moment of thoughtfulness and a little knowledge of what makes food alluring to the eye. When your dishes look beautiful, your family and guests will immediately be uplifted. More of my delightful recipes may be found in my newly published cookbook, *Celebrate Life: From the Heart of My Kitchen to Yours,* CookingwithJia@aol.com

Remember, it is the spirit surrounding food that is important. Measure your time in the kitchen and at the table by how much laughter and joy is shared.

Many Blessings, Jia

John Korpi– www.Fineartfoto.com

Perhaps because so much of our world is endangered now, appearing more fragile, more impermanent than ever before, the beauty of it can be excruciating. You know those moments, when even the most ordinary pierces the heart.

www.Joannamacy.net

Organic Farming

Organic farming is critically important to the health and future of our planet. It aids in the development of economic sustainability and enhances our quality of life in several important ways. Over the last decades, the exponential increase in the use of toxic chemicals, antibiotics and hormones in our food systems has resulted in the greatly increased contamination of our bodies, the soil, water, and air, contributing to the current environmental and health crises. In response, organic agriculture has become one of the fastest growing sectors of the economy worldwide, due to growing health and sustainability concerns from consumers and farmers alike.

Organic certification guarantees that farmers will work to minimize soil erosion, implement crop rotations, and prevent contamination of crops, soil, and water. Organic agriculture respects the balance inherent in a healthy ecosystem by encouraging wildlife, creating plant and animal diversity, building healthy soils, and conserving/protecting water resources. Organic farm management relies on developing biological diversity in the field to aid plants in developing strong immune systems, and disrupting the habitat for pest organisms, while at the same time building and replenishing soil fertility. Organic farmers do not use synthetic pesticides, herbicides or fertilizers.

Organic foods are minimally processed to maintain the integrity of food without artificial ingredients or preservatives. The Certified Organic label excludes any products that were produced with synthetic agrochemicals, irradiation, animal hormones and antibiotics and is the only way to avoid foods or ingredients that have been *genetically engineered (GMOs*, p. 8).

Organic farmers build healthy soils by nourishing the living components of the soil, (the microbial inhabitants that release, transform, and transfer nutrients). Organic matter contributes to good soil structure and water-holding capacity. Organic farmers feed soil biota, build soil structure and water-holding capacity with cover crops, compost, and biologically based soil amendments. These produce healthy plants that are better able to resist disease and insect predation, as well as, provide enhanced nutrition and *life force*. Organic farmers' primary strategy for controlling pests and diseases is prevention through good plant nutrition and management. Organic farmers use cover crops and sophisticated crop rotations to change the field ecology; effectively disrupting and reducing habitats for weeds, insects, and disease organisms.

Organic farmers rely on a diverse population of soil organisms, beneficial insects, and birds to keep pests in check; rather than continually polluting our environment with tons of toxic herbicides, pesticides and fungicides used by standard, mono-crop farming practices.

Biodynamic Farming utilizes practices that take organics to an even deeper level. Based on the teachings of Austrian philosopher Rudolph Steiner, Biodynamics is a method of agriculture which seeks to actively work with the health-giving forces of nature. It has helped pave the way for today's organic agriculture movement and is now practiced throughout the world. Biodynamics recognizes that soil itself is alive and this vitality supports and affects the quality and health of the plants that grow in it. Therefore, one of Biodynamics' fundamental efforts is to build up stable humus in the soil through composting.

Biodynamics is a science of life forces, recognizing the basic principles at work in nature, and offers an approach to agriculture which takes these principles into account to bring about balance and healing. Biodynamics is an ongoing path of knowledge and discovery rather than an assemblage of methods and techniques. We gain our physical strength from the process of breaking down the food we eat. The more vital our food, the more it stimulates our own vitality. Thus, Biodynamic farmers and gardeners aim for quality, and not always quantity.

Chemical agriculture has developed short-cuts to greater crop yields by adding soluble minerals to the soil. The plants take these nutrients via water, and short-circuit their instinct to seek from the soil what they need for health, vitality and growth. The result is a deadened soil and artificially stimulated plant growth. Biodynamics grows food with a strong connection to a healthy, living soil that dynamically relates to a healthy living body, community and world.

Conventional farming now uses 33 times more pesticides than it did 50 years ago. But crop losses are 20 times higher. That's because close to 1,000 pests have developed resistance to these synthetic toxins.

Organic Center, State of Science Report, 5/04, "Minimizing Pesticide Dietary Exposure through Consumption of Organic Food" by Charles M. Benbrook, Ph.D.

Acid / Alkaline Balance

An acidic diet creates toxicity and congestion in the body. There are three basic ways that an acidic environment in the body compromises health:

Enzymatic disturbances. Enzymes cannot function properly or, in extreme situations, cease functioning completely.

Demineralization. Minerals are lost as the body releases them in its fight to rebalance.

Overly acidic tissue. Excess acid in the tissues irritates the organs, causing inflammation, lesions, and tissue hardening.

These three factors, enzymatic disturbances, demineralization, and overly acidic tissue, can attack any organic tissue in the body, causing a wide range of illnesses. Covering up symptoms with chemicals and drugs, instead of seeking the cause of imbalance, has often led to more serious health issues.

Enzymes become compromised or ineffectual when not at a specific pH and temperature. The loss of enzyme activity affects critical areas, including assimilation of nutrients. Trying to keep bacterial balance, cellular strength, and energy without proper cellular nutrition weakens body systems.

An overemphasis on acid-forming foods (as in the typical American diet), stress, and prescription and recreational drugs compel body systems to overuse electrolyte mineral supplies to achieve balance. If the body's mineral supply is depleted, the result may be a drop of pH in the blood. The body will react by extracting buffering electrolyte minerals, first from the stomach, compromising digestion, then from other areas, including the skeleton.

In the biological terrain within the body, different microorganisms proliferate and exist in dynamic balance. When pH drops, tiny virus-like forms mutate to survive (a phenomenon called pleomorphism). They can then develop into bigger colonies of viral forms, as well as health threatening, larger bacterial and fungal forms.

When the body is acidified, extreme fatigue results. The individual often lacks drive and enthusiasm, is easily irritated, worries a lot, gets tired easily, requires a lot of rest after any exertion, and may become depressed (chronic fatigue symptoms). These symptoms

occur partly because the body diverts minerals needed for proper function, like magnesium, potassium, and calcium, to buffer the acid imbalance.

Dietary factors which create an acidic environment in the body include:

Animal proteins. This is the biggest cause of acidification of the body. Most high protein foods, especially animal foods, are acid forming. The proteins in these foods combine with sulfur and phosphorus. When protein is metabolized, these elements remain, along with uric acid from animal cellular wastes, as sulfuric and phosphoric acid. Electrolyte minerals must then neutralize these acids before the kidneys can excrete them.

The acid in animal foods is harder for the body to eliminate than that in plant foods. Animal food acids are mainly comprised of uric, sulfuric, and phosphoric acids. These acids can only be eliminated through the liver and kidneys, which can only process a limited amount each day. Excess acid is stored in the body's tissues. Plant acids—citric, oxalic, and pyruvic to name a few—once oxidized, can be eliminated through the breath. It is vital to limit or eliminate the intake of animal foods, in order to maintain a healthy acid-alkaline balance in the body.

Carbohydrate over-consumption. Excess consumption of carbohydrates, especially processed ones, stalls the multi-step process which would normally result in alkaline products, leaving acid substances in the body. Sprouted grains are alkalizing, but bread made from these grains is acidifying.

White sugar. Refined sugar and foods that contain it strain the body's defenses, because sugar is a substance that has been stripped of all its trace elements, vitamins, and minerals. The body cannot keep releasing the large amounts of trace elements and vitamins needed to convert sugar to energy, so the process inevitably breaks down and leaves sugar in one of its intermediary acidic stages. Fruit and vegetable sugars are not acidifying, because they contain all the needed vitamins, minerals and trace elements. Likewise, whole sugar, the concentrate made from evaporated sugar cane juice or sap, is not an acidifying substance.

Chlorinated water. Water normally has a pH of 7, but when highly chlorinated, it becomes acidic. Sparkling mineral water is acidic as well, due to carbonic acid used in the carbonation process.

Acid-Producing Foods

Alcohol
Beans, dried
Black pepper
Bread and crackers
Cake and pastries
Canned, frozen, or processed foods
Cereal (processed)
Chocolate
Coffee
Corn starch
Cranberries
Dairy (milk, cheese, ice cream)
Distilled vinegar
Eggs
Fish or shellfish
Fruits (processed, glazed or sulfured)
Grains (except millet, quinoa & amaranth)
Honey or molasses
Legumes (unless sprouted)
Mayonnaise or other processed
    condiments
Meat, fish or fowl
Nuts (except soaked almonds)
Oils (except flax seed or virgin olive oil)
Pasta
Plums
Popcorn
Prunes
Salt
Seeds (unless sprouted)
Soft drinks
Soy and tofu products
Sugar, saccharin, aspartame
Tea (except herbal)
Tobacco
Water (tap or carbonated)
Wheat products

Alkaline-Producing Foods

Almonds – soaked
Apple cider vinegar
Avocado
Beans, fresh
Dried fruit, non-sulfured
Fruit juice, fresh squeezed
Fruit, fresh (except cranberries)
Garlic
Green foods (algae, spirulina, chlorella,
    barley grass, etc.)
Herbal teas
Herbs
Leafy greens
Lettuce
Maple syrup
Millet, quinoa, and amaranth
Miso, tempeh
Oil (flax or extra virgin olive oil)
Potatoes and yams
Sauerkraut
Sea vegetables (dulse, kelp, arame, etc.)
Seasonings (natural, salt-free, chemical-
    free)
Seeds (flax, pumpkin, squash, sunflower
    soaked in water)
Sprouts (all types)
Stevia (natural herbal sweetener)
Miso, tempeh
Vegetable juice, freshly squeezed
Vegetable soup or broth
Vegetables, fresh (raw or cooked)
Water (purified, non-carbonated, mineral,
    or distilled)
Wheat grass juice

Colon Health

Colon Health, Toxins, and Cleansing

The choice to cleanse may come for many reasons. Sadly for many, it is often a last resort when standard medical practices have become too expensive, scary, or ineffective. This important choice is of particular value as it strengthens the immune system and is the means to assist the body in its vital natural function of elimination through open and clean channels. Once undertaken, the sense of well being, increased resistance to diseases and more positive attitude are ample reward for the challenges involved.

Our environment is dangerously full of toxins. Antibiotic resistant organisms are increasing at an alarming rate. We have become more and more alienated from our true nature, and Nature herself.

Our body's immune system and innate cleansing processes are severely compromised due to poor digestion, a diet lacking in proper nutrition, a stressful lifestyle, lack of exercise, residues of drugs, and a food supply and environment laden with toxins and chemicals. Mother Nature and our Earth are severely imperiled as global warming and toxic wastes compromise ecosystems severely.

To begin to address this situation, it is generally a good idea to start with cleansing one's own body with the aid of a holistic health coach or naturopath. Always start with the main eliminative channel, the colon. As an impaired colon becomes more open and less sluggish it is then possible to address cleansing the liver, blood, and other body systems. As one becomes less toxic and more aware, one's own ability to be part of the solution can awaken.

The main causes of impaired health directly related to the colon are sluggish digestion and constipation, which in turn are caused by:
- Lack of adequate high quality fiber in the diet
- Low probiotic population
- Lack of digestive enzymes
- Diets high in protein, particularly saturated animal fats
- Improper food combinations (see page 15)

- Overeating
- Lack of exercise
- Inadequate chewing exacerbated by excessive fluid intake with meals (Liquids are often used to wash down partially chewed food. Liquids dilute digestive juices in the stomach, and should be taken primarily between meals.)
- Impaired peristaltic (contracting) action of the colon due to toxin-related under activity of the thyroid gland and lack of thyroid-produced hormones responsible for colon movement
- Eating while feeling stressed or upset
- Eating late at night (it is best not to eat after 7:00 pm)

Sluggish digestion and constipation lead to autointoxication, as undigested food remains in the colon, putrefies and is recirculated in the body. The mucus lining of the small intestine functions like a window screen, which lets air in and keeps bugs and parasites out. When digestion is impaired, it can lead to an excessively permeable lining. This can happen when bacteria in the intestines act upon undigested food particles, producing toxic chemicals and gas. These intestinal toxins (especially from high protein animal-based foods) can damage the mucosal lining, resulting in intestinal permeability.

Once the membrane is eroded, toxins and food particles are allowed into the blood stream, where body defense mechanisms automatically store them in body fat, organs, and joints. The continued storage of toxins in body tissues can lead to compromised organ function. Common symptoms include fatigue and depression. This process is indicated as a culprit for a large number of diseases.

Other causes of colon and health problems include:

- A lack of Essential Fatty Acids (EFA) has many detrimental consequences, including compromising the liver's natural ability to break down hormones in the blood, resulting in constipation or diarrhea, and an excess of estrogen.
- Over ingestion of sugar, antibiotic use, chlorinated water, and prescription drugs all cause an increase in bad bacteria in the colon. These bacteria create toxic substances that injure the intestinal wall, contributing to intestinal permeability.

- An unbalanced diet high in processed carbohydrates, trans fatty acids, and loaded with xenobiotics (chemical compounds that are foreign to living organisms).
- Toxins and micotoxins (preservatives, pesticides, fungus, chemicals) in food and the environment that tax the colon and liver.
- Over-the-counter as well as prescription NSAIDS (Non-Steroidal Anti-Inflammatory Drugs) that irritate the digestive tract and compromise the liver's ability to cleanse.

Steps to a Healthy Bowel:

STEP 1. Lower or eliminate intake of toxins, allergenic and unhealthy foods:

Animal foods including dairy. These overload the body with saturated fat, cholesterol, protein, pesticide and herbicide residues, micotoxins, animal drugs, and hormones.

Processed food, sodas, and junk food. These contain salts, sugars, preservatives, artificial and chemically altered ingredients, hydrogenated oils, GMO, pesticides and herbicide residues and are often highly acidic.

Allergenic foods like wheat, dairy, and processed soy foods. Gluten containing foods (wheat, rye, barley), foods made with yeast (beer, yeasted breads).

Genetic Engineering. Genetic engineering is an exceedingly dangerous attempt by corporate entities to control the food supply. Many countries throughout the world have banned all genetic foods and farming practices for good reason. Interfering with the natural makeup of foods causes serious problems.

Pollen from GE strains contaminates and cross-pollinates into other regular and organic crops forever altering them and destroying their seeds.

Altering seeds and plants that have developed over ages, endangers wildlife and upsets the delicate balance of the ecology.

GE creates much more herbicide use as most of the research for genetic engineering is to make species that are tolerant of increased amounts of these poisonous chemicals.

GE is far from an exact science. Mutations and side affects can cause genetically engineered food to contain unknown toxins and allergens and also to be reduced in nutritional value.

The new genetic structure of the plant could give rise to new unusual proteins. We have no idea of there dangers and these harmful effects may not be discovered for years. Is trusting corporations—whose motives are so suspect—with your health and the stewardship of the Earth, sensible?

Caffeine, especially in coffee. Caffeine users have a much greater risk of heart attacks. Decaffeinated coffee, unless water-processed, has added dangers, specifically a high concentration of the liver carcinogen, trichloroethylene. Recent increase in the use of pesticides on coffee crops adds to the harmful effects of chemicals used to process coffee. The roasting process creates dangerous trans-fatty acids, promotes a deficiency in B vitamins, and causes continued stimulation of the adrenal glands, resulting in adrenal exhaustion and shutting down the digestive process. This in turn causes putrefaction and fermentation, turning undigested food into harmful substances. It also drives blood sugar levels up and is very acidic, leading to a decline of healthy bacteria. Green tea or Yerba Mate is a much healthier alternative.

Alcohol depletes the body, preventing or postponing normal absorption and digestion of food. The cells' ability to take in nutrients becomes impaired when alcohol is consumed, many amino acids are less easily absorbed, and more vitamins, minerals, and other nutrients are lost, creating deficiencies over time. Common allergens contained in grapes, grains, yeast, sugar, and alcohol can be allergenic, producing symptoms in the intestines and the brain. Alcohol can exacerbate yeast problems, stimulating further growth. Adverse reactions to chemicals such as sulfites used in producing alcohol are common.

Gastrointestinal problems caused by alcohol over-consumption include deficient hydrochloric acid and digestive enzymes, gastritis and ulcers, abdominal pain, "leaky gut" syndrome, esophagitis, pancreatitis, varicose veins, gallstones, and gall bladder disease. When too much alcohol is consumed, the liver stores it as fat. This causes irritation to the liver, and can eventually lead to cirrhosis or tissue scarring. The word, intoxicate, literally means "to poison." This word takes on new meaning when our goal is to detoxify the body.

Sugar is addictive and stressful on many body systems, promoting an acid environment (which causes irritation, congestion, and inflammation of the body's tissues and

eventual breakdown). Replacing real nutrition with sugary foods deprives us of needed sustenance, and depletes our tissue's health and ability to combat disease. Too much sugar in the diet can also cause hypoglycemia, problems with digestion, rapid aging, tooth decay, and has been found to be one of the strongest predictors of adult-onset diabetes. An intestinal environment resulting from a sugar-heavy diet is a perfect home for harmful bacteria, yeast, and parasites. Because of the minerals and enzymes in natural sweets such as dates and raw agave syrup they are good for food and energy, where refined sugar is good for nothing.

Salt, especially table salt with unnecessary additives such as sodium silicoaluminate, dextrose, potassium iodide, sodium bicarbonate. Unrefined mineral rich sea salt, Celtic sea salt, and Himalayan crystal salt are much better choices. (see High Vibration Foods p. 25)

Irradiated foods. Irradiating not only kills any organisms, it also destroys beneficial enzymes, quality and life force. Rotting food may be irradiated to make it saleable, though the micotoxic fecas from the organisms remains unaffected. Different research has shown irradiated food can contribute to tumors and who knows what else? This technology is basically designed to give corporations more profit and control. Eating foods the way Mother Nature created them aligns with the principle, "In God we trust."

Microwaving food, especially in plastic containers. The plastic leaches into the food. Microwaving changes the molecular structure of food.

Non stick cookware that chips plastics into food and exposes the aluminum surface underneath. Aluminum is only safe to use if coated with stainless steel.

Plastic water bottles, especially if they get warm in the car or sun. The plastic leaches into the water. Glass and uncoated stainless steel are great alternatives.

Health threatening substances such as Benzene, formaldehyde, and trichloroethylene that are found in a wide range of the environment including gasoline, particle board, dyes, bleached paper products, pharmaceuticals, inks, paints, varnishes and adhesives; also dioxins from wood preservatives and pesticides to name a few! These are known to lead to cancer, liver problems, etc.

Household cleaners, yard care products, garden products. Eliminate chemicals from your environment as much as possible. Use natural, environmentally friendly

household cleaners and natural yard care products including pesticides and herbicides as much as possible.

Trans fatty acids as in hydrogenated foods and commercial, refined oils.

Chemical/artificial sweeteners. Stevia and raw agave nectar are great natural alternatives.

Over-the-counter as well as prescription NSAIDS that compromise the liver's ability to cleanse and irritate the digestive tract.

Amalgam from mercury fillings. Find a dentist who understands the precautions needed to prevent mercury exposure during removal.

STEP 2. Clear and clean eliminative channels (Health coach):

Cleanse the colon using supplements, herbs, juicing, fasting, and raw food.

Drink plenty of liquids between meals to wash away toxins in the body (not soda). Drink plenty of clean, pure, well-filtered chlorine-free water. Do not add anything to water, like lemon, as your body will not recognize it as water. Drinking water with meals washes down food without thorough chewing.

If we don't have enough water, the body will become unbalanced. Body systems depend on the flow of nutrition and the flushing that water supports as it transports to all cells. Homeostasis and PH balance is maintained in the body's thousands of activities with the help of water. It renews the blood, supports lubrication in diverse areas such as the joints, lungs and colon, and allows the lymphatic system to cleanse. Water also supports the electrical messages constantly traveling along neural pathways.

Chew food well, as the stomach has no teeth. Taste your food; this alerts the stomach as to what is on the way, so it can provide the appropriate digestive juices. Drinking more than a few sips with meals dilutes gastric juices. Hasty eating is harmful. Starches need to be partially digested in the mouth (see Food Combining p. 15). Liquids other than water need to be swished in the mouth. Drink your food and chew your drinks. In other words, chew until your food is the consistency of baby food, and drink slowly. Give your colon an occasional rest—a day of foods blended to baby food consistency.

Consume natural fats such as sesame, coconut, and olive oil, and supplement with high Omega 3 oils such as flax, borage, and hempseed oil. Omega 3 oils have been shown to have a softening effect on the stool, to normalize bowel behavior, lower blood triglycerides (the form of fat being transported in the body), and thin the blood, thus helping to prevent clots and heart attacks.

Increase consumption of fiber rich foods and supplement with fiber products. Fiber is known to help bowel function without irritation, soften the stools allowing less straining, create regularity (correcting both constipation and diarrhea), lower cholesterol levels (reducing the harmful LDL type, while raising the beneficial HDL type), support proper blood sugar levels, and speed transit time. Minimizing transit time is vital, because the waste material has less time to feed disease-producing yeasts and bacteria. Fiber binds with toxins, including toxic chemicals, in the gastrointestinal tract and safely removes them from the body, changes harmful bacteria to a non-carcinogenic state, and removes mucus from the walls of the small intestine.

Indispensable to the health of your colon, fiber's cleansing action, antioxidant properties, nourishment of beneficial bacteria, and bulking action help protect the body from many chronic diseases. Fiber has been found to reduce the risk of breast, rectal and colon cancer, and contributes significantly to the prevention of heart disease.

STEP 3. Renew and rejuvenate with proper nutrition and health practices:

Do cleansing programs for other organs.
Eat a balanced vegan organic diet, as much as possible.
Drink a good amount of clean, pure, well-filtered, chlorine-free water daily to keep eliminative channels flowing and to maintain cellular hydration.
Supplement with a high quality EFA, a super green powder, and probiotics.
The health of the digestive tract depends on the presence of beneficial bacteria, called probiotics (pro-life).

These are the friendly bacteria of the gut and function to normalize pH of the bowel, form a healthy bowel movement, and metabolize nutrients to be more readily absorbable.

They also produce factors that prevent colonization by pathogenic (harmful) bacteria. Probiotics can help to mend the intestinal lining.

Some factors that can lower probiotic populations are acidic diets, sugar, coffee, tea, tobacco, alcohol, soft drinks, gluten containing foods (wheat, rye, barley), foods made with yeast (beer, yeasted breads), and antibiotics.

Supplements that include the amino acids L-Glutamine and N-acetyl-Glucosamine (NAG) are likewise beneficial as these amino acids are primary building blocks of the cells in the lining of the digestive track. For more information, please check in the resources section. www.VeganInspiration.com

Exercise regularly. Find activities that bring you joy.

Create a healthy sleeping environment. Use linens and bedding made from natural organic fibers, eliminating synthetic materials that off-gas while you sleep.

Consume high vibration foods. Goji berries, raw cacao, Himalayan crystal salt, maca root, Super-food Green Powder, freshly pressed juices

Find resources for local organic, seasonal fruits and vegetables. Eating what is in season in your part of the world connects you with the rhythms and cycles of the land. Farmer's markets are a great resource, and often have lower prices.

Supplement with digestive enzymes. Many foods are depleted of their natural enzymes through standard growing, processing and cooking practices. Cleansing programs catalyze healing by allowing the enzymes that, due to poor dietary practices, have been over-used, to become available to support detoxification, and to promote healing. Supplementing with digestive enzymes helps the body break down and digest food, freeing up energy for the body to work on repair. Supplementing with *systemic proteolytic enzymes* has been shown to fight inflammation, melt fibrin (fibrosis) and scar tissue, modulate immune function (antiviral), and cleanse the blood. Raw food diets, juicing and super green powders are high in enzymes and add to the body's enzyme supply.

The liver particularly benefits from enzymes, as it performs many functions, including deciphering between unwanted toxins and beneficial nutrients. The liver filters toxins from a liter of blood per minute. Toxins made up of compounds that are difficult for the liver to filter must be broken down with enzymes, so that they can be removed.

NSAIDs are a particular block to the liver's ability to remove toxins and keep harmful substances from damaging at the cellular level. Another vital function of the liver is to break down hormones. If the liver is not functioning properly due to excess fat, toxins, drugs or alcohol, an overabundance of hormones in the bloodstream can cause bloating, emotional tension and lead to some of the common severe illnesses of the sex glands. A properly functioning liver is crucial to health and detoxification.

Put more simply, humans are the leading cause of death in animals, because we unnecessarily slaughter them for food. At the same time, animals are the leading cause of death among humans, because we eat them in great excess and we pay a massive price in heart attacks, strokes, cancers, and other health problems. This is one example of the concept of pono, or supreme justice.

Dr. Terry Shintani, M.D., J.D., M.P.H. "The Hawaii Diet"™

Food Combining

Food Combining is a scientific system (Trophology) that is based on awareness of different types of digestive enzymes in the body and differing rates of digestion for particular foods. Good digestion depends on proper food combining so that the benefit of even the most healing and wonderful food is not compromised.

Starch and animal protein, the mainstay of today's typical American diet, are among the poorest food combinations. Any concentrated protein requires pepsin, which is produced by the stomach. In order for the protein to be digested fully, a highly acidic environment must be present for several hours. Starches, conversely, require an alkaline environment for proper digestion. Alkaline juices are immediately released in the mouth as soon as a carbohydrate is eaten, and this alkaline environment must be maintained in the stomach.

When full servings of protein and starch are eaten at the same time, neither one is digested properly. The body responds by producing both acid and alkaline digestive juices, which cancel each other out. The result is a thin, watery mixture that stays in the digestive tract, where bacteria cause starch to ferment and protein to putrefy. This is the main cause of many kinds of digestive problems, including gas, bloating, constipation, cramps, smelly bowel movements, heartburn, and colitis. The bacteria in the digestive tract receive the nutrition, while the body is left with the waste material. The body has a difficult time adapting when two foods with dissimilar, or opposed, digestive needs are eaten simultaneously.

In the case of whole grains that contain both starches and proteins the body is able to adjust digestive juices, both in timing and strength, to deal with a starch-protein combination, as long as it is a single food. Even then many experience difficulties with beans as they often have both. When the diet is comprised mainly of poorly combined meals, the body often produces a lot of mucus to coat toxic materials before they hurt the delicate lining of the colon.

Over time, as the body tries to deal with the continuing toxins produced by these food choices, mucus becomes impacted in the colon's folds, toxins seep into the bloodstream and the passageway for digested material becomes narrower.

The mucus impactions eventually produce pockets which press out through the colon lining. These conditions are called diverticulitis, colitis, and IBS (irritable bowel syndrome) which create an ideal environment for the next stage of colon degeneration, colon cancer.

Basic food combining guidelines

Starch and Protein—Best to avoid if possible. Combine either with vegetables for best digestion. A small amount of protein, especially plant based, added to a mainly carbohydrate meal will not be a problem, even less when lots of vegetables are eaten, providing plenty of digestive enzymes and fiber.

Acid fruit like oranges or lemons, or acids such as that in vinegar, eaten together with starch, prevent ptyalin from being produced in the saliva, and the first stage of digestion does not occur. The starch reaches the stomach without the alkaline juices needed for it to be digested correctly. The starch then comes in contact with bacteria and ferments. Sugar has the same effect when eaten with starch, preventing the production of ptyalin. This combination then blocks the sugar from moving through the stomach before the starch is digested. The sugar also ferments, leaving acidic by-products, which can further block digestion of the starch.

Starch and fat such as grains/olive oil, are a fine combination, unless something with sugar is added. Honey or jam interferes with digestion of the starch. This is also true of sugar in cereal, frosted cake, sweetened pie, etc. Natural sugar from dates and fruit are better tolerated.

Melon is a food that does not require digestion. It moves quickly through the stomach, into the small intestine, where it is digested and assimilated. However, if the stomach has anything already there, the melon is delayed in moving into the small intestine, stagnates in the digestive tract, ferments, and produces a variety of gastric symptoms.

Avoid dessert following a large meal, as this kind of food combines badly with all others. Fresh fruit is not a good alternative; it stays in the stomach, unable to be digested, and ferments.

Have salad first to support not overeating and not having lemon or vinegar with starch.

Keep it simple—not too many different kinds of protein, carbohydrate or vegetables at one meal.

Fats and Oils

Healthy fats are an important aspect of good health practices. Fats assist in proper cell construction and maintenance, as well as keeping the vital organs protected. The fatty acids in seeds store precious sunlight energy and flavorful, aromatic substances that give energy and warmth. The fat-soluble vitamins A, D, E and K need fat to be bio-available.

It's best to consume high quality, fresh fats and oils. Light and heat will quickly lessen quality, resulting in denatured oils which compromise the immune system and accelerate aging. Most commercial foods contain denatured oils, so fresh, quality oils and fats such as flax, unrefined sesame, extra virgin olive, coconut, grape seed, safflower, and hemp seed oil are best. A good test to determine the quality of any oil is to swallow a teaspoon and see if your mouth feels fresh and clean rather than acrid or coated afterwards. If the oil feels nurturing and the aroma corresponds to the food from which it was sourced, then the indications are the oil is a good quality and beneficial one.

The three different types of oils are: saturated, monounsaturated, and polyunsaturated. Within any oil there will often be a blend of one or more of these types. Butter and coconut oil are highly stable saturated fats, and are solid at room temperature. Monounsaturated oils such as olive oil thicken when chilled, but are fluid at room temperature. Flax and hemp oil are polyunsaturated fats, go rancid easily and remain liquid when chilled.

For cooking and baking, coconut oil is recommended because of its stability and fantastic flavor. If a light sautéing is needed, use grape seed, safflower oil, extra virgin olive oil and unrefined sesame oil, which withstand heat because they contain no fragile Omega-3 fatty acids. For non-cooking dishes such as salads or marinades where no heat is involved, use a favorite unrefined nut or seed oil. Find oils that have been pressed with a temperature no more than 115 degrees and that have been processed in the absence of light and oxygen using an inert gas. It is best to procure oils packaged in black, opaque, inert plastic bottles (like Omega Nutrition) to protect them from light and to make sure there is a "best if used by" date.

Refined fats are carcinogenic and suppress the immune system. Refined oils use toxic methods to strip the color, flavor and aroma of the oils to increase shelf life. High oleic oils are derived from genetically modified seeds, manipulated to decrease their essential fatty acids to increase shelf life. Expeller-pressed or pure-pressed oils are mechanically pressed at high speeds, which result in high temperatures that cause the oils to deteriorate more rapidly. Solvent extracted oils use petroleum to separate the oil from the mashed seed meal. This method is the most efficient and the least healthful. Also, refined fats often cause gastric distress, irritated lungs and mucus membranes, and rapid aging. In excess, fats or poor quality fats can burden the function of the liver and can increase cancer, Candida, tumors, cysts, edema, obesity, and some forms of high blood pressure.

Flax seed oil is one of the richest sources of Omega-3 fatty acids (along with hemp) that you can ingest. Flax tones the stomach and colon meridians. It contains up to 40 percent oil, primarily comprised of linoleic acids which are vital for strong immunity, help to prevent cancer, and keep the heart and arteries clear. Flax is also rich in lignin which is a mild estrogenic compound that helps normalize a woman's menstrual cycle, and also has anticancer, antibacterial, antifungal and antiviral properties. When soaked, flax seeds become mucilaginous (jelly-like) and are soothing. They are used as an intestinal cleanser and bowel regulator for diverticulitis and are also helpful for chronic coughing and sore throats.

Flax can also be used as an *egg replacement.* Simply grind 3 tablespoons of seeds to a fine powder in a coffee grinder and transfer to a blender and add ½ cup water, blending about a few seconds, until the mixture is gummy. This mixture will substitute 2 large eggs in any recipe. Also you can use the freshly ground flax as a nutritious condiment or supplement to smoothies and when soaked it can be easily incorporated into raw dehydrated cracker recipes.

An exceptional book on the whole spectrum of fats and oils is *Fats That Heal, Fats That Kill* by Udo Erasmus.

 # Dairy?

Milk pasteurization destroys natural enzymes, alters its delicate proteins and makes it more indigestible. Raw milk contains the active enzymes lactase and lipase, which permit raw milk to digest itself. Pasteurized milk, which is devitalized of lactase and other active enzymes, can be difficult to digest by adult stomachs, and even infants have trouble with it, as shown by colic, rashes, respiratory ailments, gas and other common ailments of bottle-fed babies. The lack of enzymes and alteration of vital proteins also renders the calcium and other mineral elements in milk largely unassimilable. People who worry about osteoporosis are often unaware that such denatured milk does not deliver sufficient calcium to prevent this condition. This is evident from the fact that American women, who consume great quantities of pasteurized milk products, suffer the world's highest incidence of osteoporosis.

Unfortunately, raw milk from well treated cows on country farms is not available, as it is illegal to sell raw milk to consumers in most states. It is much more profitable for the dairy industry to have factory farms and pasteurize milk to extend its shelf-life. Unfortunately, pasteurization renders milk from sick cows in unsanitary farms "harmless" by killing the germs, though dairy products are the most common foods recalled by the FDA for contamination with bacteria. Pasteurization also leaves the mycotoxins (excrement from bacteria, fungus and molds) and viral fragments intact.

To add to this, milk is now routinely "homogenized" to prevent the cream from separating from the milk. This process permits the tiny fragments of milk fat to easily pass through the villa of the small intestine, greatly increasing the amount of fat and cholesterol absorbed by the body. In fact, more milk-fat is absorbed from homogenized milk than from pure cream!

Today, major problems of adult infertility and early childhood body maturity are often attributed to hormones given to animals to unnaturally increase production. The medical profession is finding it more challenging to deal with the increasing failure of antibiotics due to their ingestion by humans from the prolific use of antibiotics in dairy farms to keep cows in unhealthy conditions alive.

People who abstain from dairy often have much less mucus, bronchial illness, flus and colds. These denatured dairy products gum up the intestines with layer upon layer of slimy sludge that interferes with the absorption of organic nutrients and creates the perfect breeding ground for pathogen based flus etc.

 # To Soy or Not to Soy

As vegetarian diets have gained popularity, soy has become a popular protein substitute. It has been thought that, since the Asians on the Asian diet using soy have been very healthy, that soy could be widely used as a meat substitute and made into look-alike synthetic meat products. Unfortunately this is inaccurate as the Asian diet uses only a fair amount of just slightly processed soy and owes more of its health benefits to the high content of starch, fruits and vegetables and a limited amount of animal products. It has come to light that there are some definite shortcomings to over-consumption of processed soy through the use of "fake foods" that are synthetically processed. These foods are produced by removing many of the natural substances that soy is normally made up of, leaving pure soy protein. To produce meat-like products the processed soy is then mixed with a multitude of other highly processed ingredients. Pure soy protein by itself has many problems and mixing it with other ingredients only adds to the mess.

Often babies with underdeveloped digestive systems are given formulas containing sugar, oil and concentrated soy protein. Babies will often develop allergies and have ongoing reactions to soy. This high concentration of protein from soy also leads to a high level of consumption of estrogen-like compounds.

There are many other indications of the unbeneficial effects of over-consuming soy or over-processed soy. Conversely this nutrient rich food in its near natural state is excellent, provided it is not overused. Some of the best, very simply processed soy foods are soy milk, raw miso, tempeh, edamame (boiled soy beans), and natural soy sauce such as wheat-free tamari.

> *Dick Gregory, the human rights activist and devoted vegetarian, has said that when you eat consciously and cleanse your body of toxins and fears, something truly wonderful happens: "You are really at home with Mother Nature and happily at peace with life in Mother Nature's World."*
>
> John Robbins, *The Food Revolution*

 # Why Vegan?

Avoid exposure to:
- ♥ Higher saturated fat and cholesterol
- ♥ Lack of fiber
- ♥ Higher biological concentrations of poisons in animal products
- ♥ Livestock drugs, sterols, antibiotics, growth hormones etc.
- ♥ Pathogenic micro organisms, worms, parasites
- ♥ Significant increase in heart disease risk
- ♥ Benzenes and other cancer causing compounds in cooked meat.
- ♥ Higher risk of other diseases including osteoporosis, kidney stones, diabetes, MS, arthritis, etc.
- ♥ Intestinal toxemia and slow transit time
- ♥ Excess protein that taxes organs
- ♥ Animal exploitation by factory farms.

Support:
- ♥ Much less use of fossil fuel and water
- ♥ A diet proven to be much healthier
- ♥ A diet more in harmony with nature
- ♥ More efficient use of grains
- ♥ Ecological sustainability
- ♥ Soil conservation & saving forests
- ♥ Living true to the Golden Rule
- ♥ Peace on Earth

> *The world's 1.5 billion livestock are responsible for 18% of the greenhouse gases (emissions) that cause global warming, more than all forms of transport put together. A United Nations report has identified livestock as the greatest threat to climate, forests and wildlife.*
>
> www.Earthsave.com

 # Emissaries

by Francine Hart

If you put your heart against the Earth in serving with me, in serving every creature, our Beloved will enter you from our sacred realm and we will be, we will be so happy.

Rumi

Vegan Raw Diet

Raw food has the best balance of water, nutrients and fiber to meet our body's needs. It is filled with Life Force, which nourishes us at the deepest level. It is the perfect food for us, given directly to us by our perfect Mother.

After fresh raw food is cooked above 118 degrees F for three minutes or longer, about 80% of all nutrition has been lost: 97% of the water soluble vitamins (Vitamins B and C) and up to 40% of the lipid soluble vitamins (Vitamins A, D, E and K) have been lost. Cooking makes natural fibers break down (which means it will take longer to move through the intestinal tract), protein to become coagulated (now being in a form difficult to assimilate), pesticides to be restructured into even more toxic compounds, fats to become rancid (producing free radicals in the body), and 100% of all vital enzymes to be destroyed.

When the body is given enzyme-less foods, it has to use its personal enzymes to attend to digestion, which eventually results in a reduction in the concentration of enzymes in the body called "premature aging." Enzymes are physical carriers of life energy in the body and powerful biochemical catalysts involved in virtually all processes in our body. The more enzymes are contained in our food, the less the enzyme pool of our body gets diminished and the more enzymes are available for other activities like immune system response, tissue repair, rejuvenation and healing. Preserving the enzyme pool by eating enzyme rich foods is one of the keys to lasting radiant health.

Heated, denatured food also taxes the immune system by causing the body to dramatically increase its production of white blood cells immediately following the ingestion of cooked foods. This phenomenon is called "digestive leukocytosis." The white blood cells normally defend the body against infection or poison, but their production is a routine effect of ingesting cooked foods. Could it be that the body considers such food a threat? Because leukocytes carry a variety of enzymes, another possible explanation is that white blood cells may be delivering the missing enzymes needed for proper digestion. Either way, the production of these cells creates an unnecessary stress and energy demand upon the body, eventually exhausting its vitality and strength. Leukocytosis does not occur when raw, unheated foods are eaten.

Raw food surely gives us superior nourishment, but it is important to truly understand our body and the process of the creation of disease so we can make the optimal raw food choices.

Holistic physician and pioneer researcher Dr. Gabriel Cousens states that there are only two types of bodies: bodies filled with Life force, thriving in a state of health, and bodies literally rotting, in a state of self-composting also called "chronic disease"—a state of decay eventually leading to death.

The theory of pleomorphism clearly explains how a state of disease is created in the body. This theory basically states that the secret to health is in maintaining a healthy biological terrain. Protits, which are the smallest units of life in the body, form a colloidal energy field. When this field is disrupted by toxic influences, the terrain is altered, resulting in various pathologies. Healthy protits transform, mutate into mycosis (bacteria, fungus, mold and yeast), breaking down the cells and tissues of the body and creating conditions of disease. Morbid fungal forms can also be abundantly introduced in the body through foods, mainly meat, fish, cheese, ice cream, but also peanuts, cashews, corn, and stored grains. Consider that the average American meal contains up to 1 billion pathogenic microorganisms whereas the average vegan meal contains only 500 of them. In the process of consuming our body, these morbid organisms give off waste, called "mycotoxins," which further acidify the system and encourage the growth of mycosis. This is the natural process of composting—Nature's way of recycling. There is however a way to turn off the "composting switch" and restore the body to a state of health.

Gabriel Cousens developed a diet, which he calls the "Rainbow Green Live Food Cuisine" as the optimal diet to turn off the composting switch and create and maintain health in our present times of high stress and environmental pollution. The "Rainbow Green Live Food Cuisine" is a vegan raw food diet that is non acidic, rich in sprouts, rich in greens, low in sugars, free of foods containing pathogenic microorganisms, and accompanied by healthy thoughts. Complete details including Ayurvedic principles for eating raw food are found in Dr. Cousens' excellent book, *Rainbow Green Live Food Cuisine.*

Contributed by Isabel Orr with information from Dr. Gabriel Cousens, Viktoras Kulvinskas, Antoine Béchamp, Rhio, Kouchakoff, Dr. Benarr, D.C., D.D.

High Vibration Foods

High Vibration Foods are usually grown in pristine parts of our world, in very old soil that has been maintained in sustainable ways or grown wild, and are foods that contain large amounts of phytonutrients.

Cacao: Cacao is the ancient word for the raw form of chocolate. It is the seed found in the pod-fruit of the cacao tree. It is these seeds that the Aztecs called "the food of the Gods." Cacao was so valued by the Mayans and Aztecs that it was used as money. According to David Wolfe, author of *Naked Chocolate,* cacao is the most revered of all rainforest foods. It is estimated that cacao has over 1,200 phytonutrients. Cacao is a rich source of magnesium which is much depleted in our diets today. It is also high in antioxidants, arginine (an amino acid) anandamides (the love chemical), phenyl ethylamine (PEA, the mood-enhancing phytonutrient), and cacao is considered to have many esoteric properties. This is just a small sampling of what is in cacao. For a better in-depth description of the nutrient content of cacao, history and for recipes, read *Naked Chocolate* by David Wolfe and Shazzie. Described below are the raw products derived from cacao: cacao nibs, cacao powder and cacao butter.

Cacao Nibs: Cacao nibs are the raw cacao bean with the hull removed. Removing the hull makes them easy to use. Cacao nibs can be eaten as is for a quick snack or ground into a powder using a coffee grinder or high speed blender. Ground cacao nibs can be used to make a nut or seed shake, blended into a fudge-like candy (see recipe, page 151) and made into a pudding or frozen dessert.

Cacao Powder: Cacao always refers to the raw form of chocolate and cocoa is the cooked form. Cacao powder is made by cold-pressing cacao nibs into a cake. This pressing separates the oil from the protein and fiber. The "cake-like" material that forms is cold-ground, then fine-milled and sifted, turning it into cacao powder. The best cacao powder is never allowed to get over 120° F. Keeping the product at low temperatures preserves delicate vitamins, minerals and antioxidants. David Wolfe on www.Rawfood.com states that cocoa power (the cooked form) has nearly twice the antioxidants of red wine and up

to three times more than green tea. David Wolfe's raw cacao powder tests show the raw product has fourteen times more antioxidants than red wine and twenty-one times more than green tea.

Cacao Butter: Cacao butter is the oil extracted from the cacao bean when pressing nibs for making cacao powder. White chocolate is made from it (though white chocolate is cooked). It takes three pounds of nibs to make one pound of butter. Cacao butter is one of the best skin lotions and excellent in raw desserts. When buying cacao butter, make sure it is raw, certified organic and beyond fair trade. The best quality cacao butter will have a deep golden hue and a rich delicate chocolate aroma.

Carob: Nature's First Law supplies a truly raw delicious raw carob that goes very well on its own or in combination with cacao powder. It is alkaline in nature, sweet, light and nourishing. Carob contains vitamin A and B, is rich in potassium, is 8 percent protein, and is a good source of calcium. Because carob has no caffeine or oxalic acid, which are found in chocolate, carob is often suggested as a low fat, naturally sweet substitute for chocolate.

Goji Berries: Gojies are a small coral-colored berry, that resembles raisins in size and texture, and have a super powerhouse of nutrition. Gojies are a rich source of vitamin C (over 500 times more per ounce than oranges), vitamin A, beta carotene, selenium and germanium. They also contain vitamins B1, B2, B6 and E. Goji berries also have eighteen amino acids (higher than bee pollen) including all eight essential amino acids and twenty-one trace minerals. They have a polysaccharide that is known to stimulate human growth hormone, a powerful anti-aging hormone. This wonder berry is native to the protected pristine valleys of Central Asia, primarily Tibet and Mongolia. Many of the berries are wild crafted (picked wild), others are cultivated in a sustainable way. Gojies grow on a bush-like vine that reaches over fifteen feet in length. They are air dried in the shade of their mother bush. This method of drying the berries preserves the most nutrition. Eat soaked goji berries for a quick high nutrient snack or add to smoothies, natural sweet treats and trail mixes.

The Original Himalayan Crystal Salt™: Often referred to as pink crystal salt because of its coral pink color, the Original Himalayan Crystal Salt (OHCS) is a perfect "High

Vibration Food." It comes from a time when the Earth was a pristine ecosystem. It is hand-mined, with respect for the environment, the workers, and those of us who choose this salt. A portion of the proceeds from the sale of the Original Himalayan Crystal Salt goes to support the education of the children of the area. OHCS contains 84 ionized minerals and trace elements essential to our body's health. These minerals are suspended in a colloidal form within the crystalline structure of the salt, thereby being easily absorbed and assimilated by our bodies. The elements are identical to those found in our blood and of which our bodies are made. These exact elements existed in the primal seas of our Earth, from which all life has come.

Simply speaking, life is not possible without salt in its holistic form. Whole crystal salt is more than a flavor booster. More important are its vibration or frequency patterns which are resonant to our body's own energetic make-up. All processes in the body, from the most basic to the most complex, including our very thoughts and actions, are dependent on the presence of salt in its whole, natural form. Salt is a core essential nutrient and the Original Himalayan Crystal Salt has been demonstrated to be of supreme bio-energetic value compared to the other salts we have seen.

Raw Agave Nectar: Raw agave nectar is a mineral-rich sweet syrup with a vanilla-like aroma that is used for sweetening foods. Agave nectar is harvested from living plants by Indian people native to central Mexico. Agave nectar is low on the glycemic index. The glycemic index is an indicator as to how much blood sugar levels increase in 2 to 3 hours after eating a specific food. The higher the glycemic index of a specific food, the faster it raises blood sugar levels. Look for foods low on the glycemic index such as agave nectar which is the best sweetener tested to date. Agave nectar dissolves easily in cold and hot beverages and is a great sweetener for teas and other beverages. It can be substituted for sugar in most recipes. Use ¾ cup agave nectar for each cup of sugar and reduce the liquid slightly.

Extra Virgin Coconut Oil: Coconut is one of God's greatest gifts to us. The coconut tree has been called "The Tree of Life" because it provides food, drink, building materials, can be pounded into cloth, used for fuel, and in our modern world, it has many industrial uses. Coconut oil has long been a traditional food of warm climates and today research is

proving it to be not only important as a food but as a medicine as well. Coconut oil contains about 50% lauric acid, a rare medium-chain fatty acid that is also found in mother's milk. Lauric acid makes coconut oil easy to digest, boosts the body's metabolism and gives coconut oil its antiviral and antifungal properties. These properties make coconut oil helpful for people who want to lose weight, have candida, or suffer from mold or yeast conditions. Coconut oil is white when solid and becomes a clear liquid at temperatures above 76°F. Since our bodies are 98°F, coconut oil is a liquid when ingested. When solid it is more like butter and can be used on foods in place of butter. Because it is so stable, coconut oil is one of the only oils we recommend for cooking. Buy an organic virgin coconut oil. Also, remember coconut oil can be used on the skin as it is a great moisturizer.

Young Coconuts: Young coconut is so delicious and refreshing. Its naturally sweet water, which can be drunk right out of the shell, is high in electrolytes and its pulp, a soft jell, can be scooped out for a tasty, high nutrition treat. Young coconuts have a similar pH to our blood and cell salts. They are alkalinizing to our bodies as coconut contains potassium, calcium and magnesium. Young coconut can be added to smoothies, soups, sauces and other dishes. For a powerful healing coconut juice culture, check www.BodyEcology.com

Maca: Maca, a tuber related to the radish, is cultivated high in the Andean Mountains of Peru at very high altitudes where little else grows. Maca can be eaten fresh, dried or in a powder form. The powder is what we find in the United States. Maca is best known for its powerful hormone balancing properties and as an energy booster. It has two of the essential fatty acids, linoleic and oleic acid, and contains essential amino acids as well as many other macro and micro nutrients. Some maca can be bitter. Look for the sweet tasting one like the one from Navitas, available in bulk through links on www.VeganInspiration.com

Mesquite: Native to desert areas, like the Southwest of America, mesquite is a tree that produces a bean pod with a naturally sweet, molasses-like flavor. These bean pods are milled whole into a fine meal. Mesquite is known for its antifungal, antimicrobial and antispasmodic properties. Mesquite powder can be made into a paste and used on insect bites and stings, scraps and cuts. Mesquite is one-third soluble fiber making it a slow-acting carbohydrate that has the ability to help balance and control blood sugar levels. Mesquite is

a mineral rich food perhaps because of its roots that extend deep into our Earth. Mesquite is between 14 and 16 percent protein. It mixes well with cacao and is high in the essential amino acid lysine which would tend to balance out the high arginine content of cacao.

Super Green Powders: Today we have available a bountiful selection of these powerful healing blends. Many mixtures contain a broad range of high potency extracts from the most nutrient dense, naturally occurring plant sourced ingredients. Included may be concentrated extracts from cereal grasses, algaes, sea weeds, seeds, fruits, vegetables, herbs, medicinal mushrooms and other wholesome sources. The vitamins, minerals, antioxidants, phytonutrients, probiotics and so on are very close to their natural state and therefore far more bio-available and life enhancing than many pills. Look for wild crafted and organic ingredients! Vitamineral Greens, Green Vibrance, and Perfect Food are some of the excellent ones.

> *Fortunately, more and more of us are every day realizing we can choose a way of life, and a way of eating, that free us to our highest health potential and lead us to a far more fulfilling experience of our bodies and our lives. We can experience the joy of healthy cardiovascular systems and healthy hearts, and naturally healthy blood pressure levels. We don't need any longer to clog our arteries with saturated fat and cholesterol, but can feed our bodies with wholesome natural food so we can truly live to the heights of our potential. We can break out of the habits that tell us to conform and stay put, and say No to the lies of industries that profit from our pain.*
>
> John Robbins, *The Food Revolution*

 # Ayurveda

The Science of Life and living in accordance with nature

Being that Ayurveda (pronounced eye-your-veda) is a vast and complete science of life, what is presented here is intended to be an appetizer to stimulate one's hunger for more. The goals of Ayurveda are to prevent disease, preserve health and to promote longevity. It accomplishes this by daily and seasonal routines and seasonal cleansing. Ayurveda also recommends for all body types that food be eaten as fresh as possible so that the *Ojas* or life force is still viable.

A healthier lifestyle may be skillfully created by making subtle shifts in the quality and quantity of the impressions that are consumed. The five elements that compose everything in the universe are: space, air, fire, water and earth. Space lives as the actual spaces in the body, the colon, in the ears, the space between breaths, etc. Air circulates blood through the heart and governs her rhythms and moves the breath, nutrition, emotion and elimination. Fire lives in the body as passion, heat and ability to digest and transform. Water is all the fluids, while earth is the structure, bones, tendons, cartilage and muscles. These five elements come together to form the three body types or *doshas* of *vata, pitta* and *kapha.* Vata is composed of space and air. It is cold, dry, light, rough, mobile, subtle and clear having the governing principle of movement. Pitta is composed of fire and water. It is hot, moist, mobile, light, sharp and penetrating and has the governing principle of transformation. Kapha is made up of water and earth and the governing principle is structure. It is cold, heavy, dense, cloudy, slimy, oily and soft. People are a combination and permutation of the three doshas, five elements and twenty qualities.

Vata. Primarily Vata people have a thin frame, delicate constitution, tend to be flat-chested, have difficulty gaining weight and are easily excitable. Vata derangement can lead to the following disorders: sensitive nervous system, gas and bloating, irregular or weak digestive energy, vertigo, sciatica and challenges and pains in the muscles and joints. Vata does best with a warming diet composed of strengthening and grounding foods that moisten and lubricate. Flavors that benefit vata are sweet, salty and sour.

Prefer: Vata people would want to take foods that are warming, unctuous, oily, liquid and grounding with tastes that are sweet, salty and soupy and moderately pungent. Fats and oils warm, lubricate and help ground vata people providing they are unrefined and used moderately. Sesame oil is the most balancing for vegans, and according to Ayurveda Ghee is highly recommended for vata people, followed by almond oil, extra virgin olive oil and coconut oil. To make salads more easy to assimilate, add an oil-rich dressing and digestion-enhancing herbs. Nuts and seeds are moistening, heavy and warming and nourish vata as long as they're taken in small easy-to-digest quantities. Drink warm herbal teas such as chai. Herbs and spices benefit vata as they aid digestion and help dispel gas. They are especially beneficial added to sweet or heavy foods and include: asafoetida, basil, bay leaf, cardamom, cinnamon, cloves, coriander, cumin, fennel, fenugreek, fresh ginger, mace, marjoram, nutmeg, oregano, savory, thyme and turmeric. It is also important for vata to eat at regular intervals in a warm, comfortable, calm setting and center or meditate before eating.

Avoid: It is particularly important for vata people not to rush or talk excessively during meals. Avoid: dry, cold, pungent (in excess), bitter and astringent foods. Hot spices such as dried ginger, chilies or mustard, dry fruits (unless they are soaked), watermelons, apples, granola, cold breakfast cereals, crackers, chips, rice cakes, popcorn, chips, crusty or yeast bread, dried grains, celery, eggplant, mushrooms, tomatoes and white potatoes.

Pitta. Pitta people are hot-blooded, passionate individuals with strong, fast digestive systems and an ability to digest anything. Pitta's are often seen as muscular with unlimited energy and strength, though they can burn out easily without regular meals and getting to bed at a reasonable time.

Prefer: Since this dosha is hot, oily and light, it does best with a diet that is cooling, slightly dry and more grounding, favoring mildly spiced low salt, foods with flavors that are sweet, bitter and astringent. Cooling herbs and spices like cardamom, cilantro, cinnamon, coriander, cumin, fennel, mint, parsley, and turmeric are best for pitta. Astringent and cooling beverages such as apple and pomegranate,

vegetable juices, green drinks such as wheat grass juice or spirulina and spring water. Alfalfa, raspberry leaf and green tea are all especially cooling in the summertime. Sweet tasty fruits like apples, and pears tend to cool and calm pitta and relieve thirst. Grains strengthen, but do not overeat them. Sunflower seeds and soaked and peeled almonds are cooling and nourishing for pittas.

Avoid: Hot, spicy, oily foods, caffeine, excess salt, alcohol, beer, wine, sour (grapefruits, lemons, sour cherries and plums), nuts, seeds and their oils are warming and therefore best used in moderation by pittas.

Kapha. Kapha people tend to be those who gain weight easily and have incredible stamina, strength and longevity. They have a heavy bone structure with wider shoulders and hips and they are known by there easy-going and complacent personalities. They tend to have problems with their lungs, being overweight, congestion and colds/flu. It is important for this type to eat less food less frequently as their digestion is usually slow.

Prefer: The best food choices for kaphas include foods that are light, warm and dry. They do well with raw, and are greatly benefitted by bitter and astringent greens and heating spices and foods; beans and legumes, green and black tea and coffee occasionally. Also beneficial are ginger, chicory or dandelion teas, soy milk, drying diuretic grains such as amaranth, barley, buckwheat, corn, millet, dry oats and teff. Include digestion enhancing herbs and spices such as asafoetida, basil, black pepper, black mustard seeds, chilies, coriander, cumin, galangal, fresh and dried ginger, fennel and fenugreek. Seeds (mainly flax, pumpkin and sunflower) are preferable to nuts. Limited use of coconut and almonds is okay.

Avoid: Avoid fatty fried foods, dairy, sweet, sour and watery vegetables, excess fluids, iced and chilled beverages.

> *When the ahara (food that one takes in from the outside either physically or mentally) is pure, then the mind becomes pure. When the mind becomes pure, the smirti (or memory of one's Divine nature) becomes constant and one's heart becomes free from knots and bondages.*
>
> The Upanishads, translated by Juan Mascaro

Yogic terms also classify foods and all of creation by their energy. The three Gunas, or qualities of nature, are *rajasic*—activating, *tamasic*—evil, obstructing, and *sattvik*—good, expanding.

For more information and a deeper understanding of Ayurveda please contact *contributing co-author, Darci Frankel, a skilled Ayurveda practitioner/educator, owner of Hanalei Day Spa and Ayurveda Center of Hawai'i on Kauai, and facilitator of Pancha Karma cleansing and rejuvenation programs.* www.PanchaKarma.net

"Darci has a strong commitment to healing and transformation which she expresses through her wisdom in Ayurveda." **Deepak Chopra M.D.,** author, *The Path to Love*

Krishna's Three Classes of Food

Foods that promote longevity, vitality, endurance, health, cheerfulness, and good appetite, and that are savory, mild, substantial, and agreeable to the body, are liked by pure-minded (sattvik) persons.

Foods that are bitter, sour, saltish, excessively hot, pungent, harsh, and burning are preferred by rajasic men, and produce pain, sorrow, and disease.

Foods that are nutritionally worthless, insipid, putrid, stale, refuse, and impure are enjoyed by tamasic persons.

God Talks with Arjuna, The Bhagavad Gita,
Royal Science of God Realization, Paramahansa Yogananda,
Self-Realization Fellowship, LA, California

In creation it appears that God sleeps in the minerals, dreams in the flowers, awakens in the animals and in man knows that He is awakening.

Sayings of Yogananda, Paramahansa Yogananda
Self-Realization Fellowship, LA, California

 # Fasting & Meditation

Empowering Insightful Awareness

Meditation, fasting and a lighter, cleansing diet are often conducive to physical, emotional, and mental healing, and spiritual revelation. These practices can strengthen and develop personal will power, give our organs a needed rest, and free the life force to focus on repair and rejuvenation. Outstanding results have been achieved with fasting in reducing blood pressure and reversing potential life-threatening atherosclerosis as well as efficacious outcomes with a myriad of other ailments.

"Fasting can save your life by enabling you to cheerfully and enjoyably adopt a diet and lifestyle consistent with your natural design, one that will protect your health by preventing unnecessary disease. It is this ancient and natural process that may enable you to escape from modern life's most deadly and insidious force: the drug like allure of modern foods—the dietary pleasure trap." Further fasting information available at www.thepleasuretrap.com, www.treeoflife.nu and www.optimumhealth.org

Many "Wisdom Traditions" are congruent in their precepts of a simpler, less harmful diet, combined with wholesome living and self-discovery practices to support insightful awareness meditation. Practices of non-attachment/aversion, mindfulness and being present can help one open to the roots of their own suffering, allowing the feeling of how all suffer, which opens the doors of forgiveness, generosity and faith. As discriminating intelligence and skillful awareness guide our actions, delusional hindrances, emotional afflictions and instinctive propensities developed over time no longer unconsciously seduce us into acts that cause us more suffering. A life based on fear, anger, attachment, and control can transform to dedication to the happiness of all beings, loving kindness, sympathetic joy and equanimity.

As awareness and non-participation in patterns of conflict conditioning deeply rooted/obscured in our personality arises, so our authentic inner peace and clarity develop. From this self-actualized perspective, the dream of a harmonious Earth becomes integrated as does one's ability to disengage from old, outmoded paradigms and effectively participate in skillful new life-affirming creations.

Rainbow Fusion

Rainbow Fusion Cuisine is the conscious integration of intentional choices, principles, and practices to alchemically infuse, and synergistically instill, maximum coherent resonance, life-force and love into food. This results in an experience of food as a communion, vibrantly wholesome, that nurtures the seven chakras (energy centers), supporting harmony within ourselves and unity with all life.

It is important to choose high quality, organically farmed products, where nature and the interconnectedness of all life are honored. It also makes a considerable difference what we support when we spend money. In effect, we are "voting with our dollar" either to care for the environment, or for non-sustainable practices that endanger our health and poison our Earth. Dishes may be prepared to be full, round, soft and complex, playfully contrasting textures and tastes. Many recipes intermingle sweet and tart tastes, progressing to a burst of peppery heat, accentuating spicy or fresh fragrant herbs to add a flavorful, tantalizing high note. Healthy cooking practices, like not over-cooking and serving fresh food, keep the life force intact. Personal energy in preparing and serving food can have a dramatic effect. Superlative results are attained when the meal is prepared in a loving, grateful way. Lighthearted conversing, focusing on uplifting subjects, and singing, with harmonious music or spiritual chants will intrinsically influence the energetic resonance within the meal (most likely due to positively effecting water crystalline structure as outlined in Masuru Emoto's book, *Messages from Water*). Including different colored foods adds beauty, aesthetic appeal, and healthy rainbow phyto-nutrients. Dedicating the fruit of one's labor to the Divine and a prayer of thankfulness add the final loving touches. Food prepared this way has been commented upon as being effulgent or radiating an appealing light.

Sacred symbols reflect this interconnection of creation as Aum (OM) is the signifier of the ultimate truth that all is one and also reflects the triune energies of disillusion (Shiva-A) sustaining (Vishnu-U) and creation (Brahma-M).

The Sri-yantra is also a graphic representation of the underlying universal processes and shows the actual proportional series that govern the relationship of the notes with the musical scales

"Healing the Heart"

www.FrancineHart.com

The new solution to Einstein's equations generates tetrahedral structures fundamental to creation and our existence in it.

Physicist Nassim Haramein, www.theresonanceproject.org

Foundational Wholistic Health Practices

Consume predominately organic, vegan, pure whole foods, that have a minimum of processing, are locally grown, and are in season, whenever possible!

Healthy cooking and dietary practices:
- Proper food combining and balancing of proteins, carbohydrates, fruits, vegetables, fats and sweets, acid to alkaline.
- Use of beneficial non-rancid cold-pressed oils like olive, sesame, safflower, grape seed and raw coconut.
- Minimizing use of sugar, caffeine and alcohol.
- Eating a high percentage of raw foods (at least 60%).
- Intake of enough fiber—fruits, vegetables, flax formulas to support acid alkaline balance, regularity and colon health.
- Sprouting or soaking nuts and seeds to release enzyme inhibitors.
- Minimizing consumption of simple carbohydrates such as flour products.
- Having a smoothie or fruit dish full of nutritional support in the morning.
- Drinking freshly made vegetable juice in the afternoon.
- Drinking 2 to 3 quarts of clean, pure, fresh, filtered or spring water, daily.
- Awareness of allergenic foods like dairy, wheat and processed soy products.
- Discontinue ingestion of chemically altered foods, trans-fatty acids, hydrogenated oils, preservatives, GMO, food colorings, chemical sweeteners.
- Get regular, aerobic exercise to increase oxygen and circulation.
- Use of professionally overseen cleansing programs to remove congestion and toxins, starting with the colon and going on to rebuild organs and glands.
- Sensible supplementation to add necessary factors to a vegan diet including: extra supplementation with nutrient dense green powder super foods, high vibration foods (raw cacao, maca, gogi berries, Himalayan crystal salt, bee pollen), hemp protein powder, and probiotics. Herbal preparations and natural therapies whenever possible rather than pharmaceuticals. Systemic and digestive enzymes, essential fatty acids from hemp, flax, borage or evening primrose oils.
- Practices such as Yoga for flexibility, strength and inner peace.

Recipe Guidelines & Hot Cooking Tips

Please read through the book first, before trying the recipes, especially the glossary of definitions and terms. There is a wealth of pertinent information throughout the book to support the creation of beautiful meals.

1. Use the freshest, least processed, organically grown products and produce available. Buy locally grown whenever possible.
2. Read the recipes all the way through, making sure all the necessary kitchenware and ingredients are on hand.
3. Many ingredients, especially types and quantities of vegetables, are approximate. When crucial, the recipe will specify. Strong herbs, such as nutmeg and baking ingredients, like baking powder, are most sensitive to quantities.
4. Adjust seasonings to personal taste. For soy-free diets, soaked nuts, crystal salt, and Umeboshi vinegar may be substituted for soy products in many recipes. For transition diets, the protein sources in recipes may be adjusted.
5. It's better to add miso (unpasturized) at the end, when cooking is completed, in order to protect miso's live enzyme content.
6. Use filtered or fresh spring water.
7. It is best to cook in a calm, stress-free environment. Projecting loving thoughts around food can have a noticeable effect on the vibration and quality of the meal. Cooking with friends, and sweet, uplifting background music or chanting add more sweet energy to food.
8. A food processor is excellent for quickly chopping large amounts of peeled ginger or garlic. A coffee grinder that is not used for coffee, may be used in place of a mortar and pestle to grind herbs, flax seeds, gogi berries, etc.
9. When testing flavors, a small dab on the back of the wrist works well rather than using multiple spoons or putting a used utensil back in the food.
10. Serve food with artistic flair. Exquisitely balanced dishes can be created by including a variety of colors: purple cabbage, red pepper, orange carrot, and edible flowers; textures like creamy, crunchy and chewy; and tastes like sweet, sour, spicy, salty, bitter. Salads may be made into works of art (see Mandala Salad pictures on inside covers).

Above all, let your own creativity and enthusiasm guide your creations!

Common Shopping List Items

Fruits
Apples
Bananas
Berries
Citrus fruits
Dates (also a sweetener)
Dried apricots
Figs
Lemons
Mangos
Melons
Papayas
Pineapple
Prunes
Raisins
Stone fruits

Salad Vegetables
Avocado
Beets
Carrots
Celery
Clover sprouts
Cucumber
Edible flowers
Exotic salad mix
Jicama
Lettuce
Mung bean sprouts
Olives
Red & green onion
Red cabbage
Red pepper
Romaine lettuce
Sunflower sprouts
Tomatoes

Fresh Herbs
Basil
Cilantro
Dill
Oregano
Parsley
Rosemary
Thyme

Sea Vegetables
Agar Agar
Arame
Dulse
Kelp
Kombu
Nori

Cooking Vegetables
Broccoli
Carrots
Cauliflower
Chard
Collards
Daikon
Garlic
Ginger
Green beans
Kale
Onion
Spinach
Zucchini

Proteins
Almonds & almond mylk
Black beans
Protein powder, hemp or rice
Red lentils
Raw tahini
Raw almond butter
Seeds & nuts
Soy products – soy milk,
Westbrae Soy-Rice, or
    Light-life Garden
        Vegetable tempeh blocks
        and tempeh bacon
Tofu
Quinoa
Nutritional yeast
Green powders
Hemp protein powder

Starches
Ezekiel bread, tortillas &
    bagels (whole grain)
Kabocha and other squashes
Quinoa, red and white
Red, white & purple potatoes
Garnet yams
Rice – wild, brown or white
    Basmati, or short grain
Purple "Forbidden Rice"

Oils, Condiments, Spices
Coconut milk – Thai Kitchen
Oils: Coconut, olive, safflower,
    sesame & grape seed
Mustards: Dijon & stone ground
Vegan veggie stock cubes & powder
Sea salt, crystal salt, tamari
Vegenaise
Vinegar: apple, Balsamic, or ume
Miso: unpasturized white or brown
Thai Kitchen "Spicy Chili Sauce"
Mae Ploy yellow curry paste
Sun dried tomatoes (also smoked)

High Quality Seasonings:
Cumin, curry, cardamom, thyme, oregano,
    cinnamon, coriander, pepper, taco
    seasoning, nutmeg, allspice, red chili
    pepper, caraway, vanilla
Organics: All purpose seasoning,
    garlic pepper & salt, Spike

Super Foods
Bee pollen
Green Powders
Hemp, Borage & Flax oils
Nut mylks, fresh sprouted
Raw cacao
Gogi berries
Raw fresh vegetable juices
Maca powder

Medicinal Herbs
Grapefruit seed extract
Green papaya powder
Slippery elm bark powder
Tea tree oil

Sweeteners:
Agave nectar (raw)
Brown rice syrup
Raw organic honey
Maple syrup
Rapadura
Stevia, xylitol (no sugar)
Sucanat

Not to live to eat, or eat to live, but to eat in order to enhance one's communion with the Divine.

Gabriel Cousins, *Sevenfold Peace*

Basic Kitchen Tools and Measurements

Tools

Apron - always handy and a good idea.

Pots - stainless steel with glass lids, if possible. Sizes: 2-gallon, 1-gallon, 2-quart, 1-quart and ½-quart.

Pans - 2 heavy-duty nonstick, 1 large and 1 medium size.

Steamer basket or electric steamer.

Measuring cups and spoons.

Mixing bowls - 2 large & 2 medium.

Baking dishes - 1 large & 1 medium rectangular glass dishes, 1 round glass pie plate.

Appliances

Blender and/or Vita Mix or K-Teck

Food processor - Cuisinart is the best. Lower priced brands are noisier and less smooth but work fine

Coffee grinder - has many uses: grinding herbs, seeds, or coarse salt.

Champion or other juicer

Lemon juicer - electric or glass.

Salad spinner - pull string or top button models work best.

Utensils

Garlic press, ginger grater, large standing vegetable grater, potato masher, cutting boards, wire whisk, large & small volume screen sieve, vegetable peeler.

Cutlery

Knives - high quality small, medium, and large with some serrated.

Wooden stirring spoons, flexible plastic scraping spatula, stainless and rubber cooking spatulas, stainless steel ladle and serving spoons, tongs, wooden rice paddle, salad servers.

Serving Sizes

2½ C uncooked rice / quinoa = 1 pound

1 C cooked rice or quinoa is considered one serving.

1 C grain cooked with 2 C water makes 3 servings of 8 oz each.

12 oz bowl of soup = one serving

10 oz of stew or curry = one serving

1 oz of thick salad dressing = 1 serving

1 medium orange = ¼ C of orange juice

Measurements

3 tsp (teaspoons) = 1 T (tablespoon)

2 T = 1 oz (ounce)= ⅛ C

5 T + 1 tsp = 1/3 cup

8 oz = 1 C (cup)

4 T = ¼ C

2 C = 1 pint

2 pints = 1 quart

4 quarts = 1 gallon = 16 cups

Dining As Communion

10 ways to create the healthiest, most nurturing experience of food.

- Always give thanks to the Source for the gifts and abundance of life. Grace imbues the meal with love and thankfulness.
  Many are hungry; gratitude leads to compassion.
- Eat in a state of peace. If necessary rest, exercise or meditate to regain center.
- Keep dinner conversations lighthearted; remember to chew each mouthful thoroughly, enjoying the aromas, textures, flavors and tastes.
- Eat simply; don't eat too much or have too much variety.
- Eat food that is not too hot, too cold or overcooked.
- Eat moderately and slowly. Chopsticks work well for this.
- Minimize the intake of liquids at, or after, meals—as the digestive fire is diluted by liquids and slowed by cold.
- If having dessert, wait for a while after the meal.
- Eat when hungry, and minimize between-meal snacks.
- Eat at regular times, and as early in the evening as possible, to allow three or more hours for complete digestion before bedtime.

Healing practices followed by Hawaiian ancestors:

They ate together (aloha).
They ate in peace (mana).
They said a prayer before eating (pono).
They ate foods in season (lokahi).
They ate foods from their locality (lokahi).
The food was prepared with love (aloha).
The food was eaten with great appreciation of its source (kumu).

Dr. Terry Shintani, M.D., J.D., M.P.H., "The Hawaii Diet"

 # *Grace*

The conscious and loving preparation of food is both a Holy Art and Divine Alchemy. When infused with love and awareness, food becomes manna and medicine for our bodies and our souls. Through the simple, yet essential, act of eating, we have the power to uplift or diminish, heal or destroy (make or break) bodies, souls, civilizations, worlds…

In the sublimely subtle and intricate interconnectedness of all life, we exist as part of an exquisitely beautiful and delicate web. All life forms feed and are fed from each other. How conscious we are of this interplay determines our ultimate wellbeing and happiness. It is the deepest truth and highest ecstasy to experience ourselves as One with all there is. This awakened awareness is the fulfillment of our existence. It is the sublimely embodied Presence of the One Divine Being.

To have a relationship with all life as if all were your Beloved, because in truth it is, is an invitation to each of us. How do we walk upon the Earth so lightly, tenderly, and compassionately as to leave no foot print that is not a blessing and a prayer? Only in and as love can we do this, for love is the truth of who we are. So it is that every moment, every breath, intention and action becomes an opportunity to bring through more love into form.

Ideally we would all eat pure and simple from the Earth, from gardens and orchards grown with Love, harvest the food with Love, prepare it with Love, and eat it with Love, gratitude and joy in our hearts. Our very handling of the food with Love imparts the most subtle, yet essential qualities to its nature, and surely it is what really determines the outcome of any recipe.

Composed by Grace, for my Beloved friend Vegananda, Kealakekua Bay, Hawaii, April 2005

> *Compassion is the foundation of everything positive, everything good. If you carry the power of compassion to the marketplace and the dinner table, you can make your life really count.*
>
> Rue McClanahan, quoted in *May All Be Fed,* John Robbins

Recipes

Rainbow Fusion Cuisine for Body, Mind and Spirit

Blessing Prayer / Grace

Artistic Visual Presentation

Harmonious Music and Chanting

Heartfelt Care and Service

Wise Cooking Practices and Ingredients

Tantalizing Flavors and Textures

Organic, Vegan Whole Foods

 # Beverages

Apple Cider and Spice
4 servings

4 C apple juice
1 3" cinnamon stick
½ tsp whole cloves
½ tsp cardamom seeds
¼ tsp nutmeg, grated
¼ tsp coriander seeds
Opt: sweetener; 2 T maple syrup
   and ¼ C lemon juice

In a 1½ quart pot bring apple juice and herbs to a low boil.
Cover and reduce to low and simmer for 20 minutes
Strain out the spices and add sweetener if desired.
Lemon juice may also be added for a tangier drink

Hip Hemp Mylk
2 servings

2 C water
½ C hemp seeds
1 T raw cacao powder
1 tsp maca powder
2 tsp agave nectar
Opt: 1 tsp super green powder

Put water and hemp seeds in a blender and run on high speed for one half minute. Add rest of ingredients and blend well.
Endless variations are possible with the exemplary base of hemp seeds and water!

To awaken within the dream is our purpose now. When we are awake within the dream, the ego created earth drama comes to an end and a more benign and wondrous dream arises. This is the new Earth.

Eckhart Tolle, *A New Earth*

Nut and Seed Mylks

makes about 4 cups

½ C raw almonds or other nuts and/or seeds
2 C water
⅛ tsp crystal salt
Opt: 1 tsp vanilla extract,
     dates or agave nectar for sweetening to taste

Put the nuts and/or seeds into a jar, cover generously with filtered water and soak nuts 8 to 12 hours and seeds 2 to 4 hours. If the nuts or seeds are white, such as cashews, pine nuts or white sesame seeds, the shorter time is fine. Discard the soaking water and thoroughly rinse the nuts and/or seeds.

For almonds only: to make a smoother mylk, blanch and remove their skins. To blanch, in a sauce pan bring 2 cups of water to a boil. Have almonds in a bowl and immediately cover them with the boiled water for 1 minute. Drain then plunge the almonds into cold water. Squeeze the almonds between your fingertips to remove their skins. Discard the skins.

In a blender, put the soaked nuts and/ or seeds and all the remaining ingredients and blend into a mylk-like consistency.

Strain (Optional): Nut and seed mylks can be used as is or strain for a smoother texture. If using brown sesame seeds or unblanched almonds, straining is recommended. To strain, pour the nut or seed mixture into a large stainless steel mesh food strainer and press out the liquid with the back side of a wooden spoon.

Nut and seed mylks will keep for about 3 days in the refrigerator, except for sesame mylk which keeps its mellow flavor for about 2 days.

Other Options: 2 dates can be substituted for the agave nectar. Cacao or carob powders can be added before blending for chocolate or carob mylk.

Basic Almond Mylk

4 servings
This is an enzyme-rich, nutrient-dense, extra-delicious mylk.

½ C almonds, soaked 12 hrs
  (= 1 C after soaking)
3 C filtered water
3 dates, pitted
Opt: 1 tsp vanilla

Drain almonds and blend with water for 1 minute on high. Pour mixture through a strainer and press out the mylk, discarding the pulp.
Add liquid back into blender with dates and vanilla and blend until well mixed.

This mylk will keep in an airtight container in the fridge for 3 days.
Drink as is or use in salad dressings or in raw soups.

Spicy Nut Mylk

4 large servings

4 C nut mylk (p. 47)
2 C water
2 T fennel seeds

½ tsp cardamom seeds
1 T minced ginger
4 whole cloves
½ C dates pitted

Bring water to a boil, add spices, cover, lower heat and simmer for 10 minutes, remove from heat and let cool.
Blend dates with 1 C mylk. Strain out spices from water and mix well with remaining mylk.
Excellent served warm!

Almond Nog
2 servings

½ C raw almonds, soaked 12 hours
½ C dates soaked 2 hours in 3 C water
1 tsp pure vanilla
½ tsp cinnamon powder

1 pinch ground nutmeg
1 pinch crystal salt
¼ C cacao or carob powder, optional

Blend almonds with dates, soak water and pour through a cheesecloth, sprout bag
or strainer. Return to blender, add all ingredients and blend well.
For best flavor warm and serve immediately!

Awesome Sesame Milk
2 servings

¾ C unhulled sesame seeds
soaked 3-4 hours in 2 C water

2 C and 1½ C pure water

Rinse sesame seeds and add with 2 cups fresh water to a blender.
Blend on high speed for 1 minute. Pour through fine mesh 6" sieve into a bowl
and lightly press with spoon to squeeze out liquid.
Return to blender with remaining 1.5 C water and repeat process.
Excellent used in smoothies, salad dressings and fruit salads.
Lasts 2-3 days in a well sealed container in the fridge.
Optional: Blend 1-2 T hemp seeds into milk.

If you want to know what health is worth, ask the person who has lost it.

John Robbins

Almond Fruit Lassi
4 servings

½ C raw almonds, soaked, blanched
   and skins removed
3 C water
2 C diced mango, peach, apricot or
   banana, fresh or frozen
2 T agave nectar or other sweetener
½ tsp cinnamon powder
¼ tsp cardamom powder
Opt: 2 T raw almond butter

In a blender, put all the ingredients
and blend until creamy smooth. If too
thick, add a little more water.

Mango Lassi
2 servings

2 C soy (or other) mylk
1 C mango, chopped
1 tsp cardamom
2 dates, pitted or
1 T maple syrup

Blend all ingredients together to make
a creamy, delicious Indian-style drink.

> *Most of the nations that now import grain from the United States were once self-sufficient in grain. The main reason they aren't any longer is the rise in meat production and consumption.*
>
> John Robbins, *May All Be Fed*

Amma Chai
2 servings

4 C water
2 T coarsely grated fresh ginger
1 T cardamom pods, crushed
1 T dried orange peel (organic)
1 T whole black peppercorns

6 whole cloves
2 cinnamon sticks, about 3" long
4 T peppermint tea or Darjeeling tea
agave nectar or other sweetener to taste
vanilla soy mylk, to taste

Add all ingredients in a large sauce pan (except the peppermint or Darjeeling tea and sweetener or mylk), cover and simmer for 10 minutes. Remove from the heat, add the peppermint or Darjeeling tea, cover and steep for 3 to 5 minutes. The longer the tea steeps the stronger it will be and left too long it will become bitter. Strain out the spices and tea leaves and add sweetener and mylk to taste.

Matisha– www.songofhome.com

Lokah, Samastah, Sukino, Bhavantu, May All Beings Be Happy!

Amma Chi

51

Hot Coconut Carob
2–3 servings

3 C nut or soy mylk
3 T carob powder
4 pitted dates, soaked if needed
pinch crystal salt

½ tsp pure vanilla extract
1 T coconut oil
Opt: pinch of red pepper

Blend all ingredients until smooth.
Gently warm and serve.

Indian Chai
4 servings

4 C water
1 T cardamom pods
1 T ginger root, fresh grated
1 tsp whole cloves
1 tsp black peppercorns
3" cinnamon stick
2 green, black, or maté tea bags

Boil together all (except tea bags) for
15 minutes.

Add bags and steep 3 more minutes.
Strain spices and serve with mylk and
sweetener of choice.

*OM ASATOMA SATGAMAYA, TOMASOMA JYOTIR GAMAYA,
MRITYORMA AMRITAM GAMAYA*

*Hindu Mantra: to assist shifting from the false to the truth,
from the darkness to the light, and from poison to nectar.*

Noni Sun Tea

10 noni fruit—turning white or almost soft

Simply place noni in a 1 gallon covered glass jar in partial sun. As noni ripens, it will exude a golden colored tea. Drink 1 to 2 ounces first thing in the morning on an empty stomach. It is recommended to do 5 days on and 5 days off. This is a very powerful blood cleanser and detoxifier. Use consciously. Optional additions: aloe vera juice, grated ginger, Kombucha tea, a touch of honey to sun tea. Fresh squeezed noni pulp may be created by pressing fresh ripe nonis through a fine colander to remove seeds. Pulp is excellent to eat or use in dressings, etc..

In the degree that we recognize our oneness, our connection, with the Infinite Spirit which is the life of all, and in the degree that we open ourselves to this divine inflow, do we come into harmony with the highest, the most powerful, and the most beautiful everywhere.

Ralph Waldo Trine, *At Home in the Universe*

Basic Fresh Juice
2 + servings

1 lb carrots
1 medium beet
¼ lb kale (or other greens)
1 cucumber
4 stalks celery
1" ginger, peeled and chopped
1 small bunch parsley
Opt: 1 clove garlic
   ½ green apple

This recipe requires the use of a juicer.

Wash all vegetables. Trim carrot ends. Cut celery, cucumber, and beets into quarters.

For ease of juicing, alternate the greens with the other veggies.

Drink within ten minutes for full vitality! A delicious, nutritious treat. Add other vegetables of choice. If you are sensitive to sugar, use less carrots and more greens.

The factory farming techniques of present-day civilization have created a frightening Karmic debt and health danger for anyone still consuming flesh foods—especially if eaten raw. Factory-farmed animals are injected with, sprayed with, and fed antibiotics, artificial hormones, chemicals of all kinds, and genetically-modified foods; these toxins are present in the flesh when the animals are slaughtered; they are passed directly into the body of the flesh consumer.

David Wolfe, *The Sun Food Diet Success System*

Lean Green Juice
2 servings

4 leaves romaine lettuce
2 green apples
2 stalks celery
½ C parsley
1 un-waxed cucumber
½ C spinach

Juice all the ingredients together.
Serve in fancy glasses.

Ingredient Notes: To make this a *really* chlorophyll-rich drink, add spirulina. If you want even more calcium in this drink, add carrot juice to taste.

Super Alkalinizing Juice
2 hefty servings

1 lb carrots, peeled
3 stalks celery
2 beets
¼ head cabbage

¼ bunch parsley
1 clove of garlic
1 green apple may be added for flavor

Juice together.

An individual, has not begun to live until he can rise above the narrow confines of his individualistic concerns to the broader concerns of all humanity.

Martin Luther King Jr., *At Home in the Universe*

Garden Favorite Smoothie

2 servings

1 medium papaya, ripe
1 frozen banana
1 medium mango, chopped
1 C rice mylk
1 C water or fresh coconut water
1 T Green Vibrance powder

1 T rice protein powder
1 T hemp protein powder
1 T bee pollen
1 tsp green papaya powder
1 T flax seeds, ground
1 tsp slippery elm powder

Love Potion Smoothie, (Breakfast of Champions!)

2 servings

2 C fresh almond or sesame mylk
1 ripe banana or papaya
½ C frozen berries
¼ C goji berries soaked in sesame
  mylk 2 hours
2 tsp coconut oil, raw-virgin

1 T Vita mineral greens
2 T raw cacao powder
2 T hemp protein powder
1 T bee pollen
1 T hemp seeds
1 T maca powder

May also be added into a wonderful fruit salad with chopped apples etc.
Fondly named "Magic Mush or Breakfast of Champions."

This we know. The Earth does not belong to man: man belongs to the Earth. This we know. All things are connected like the blood, which unites one family. All things are connected.

Chief Seattle's Address, 1854

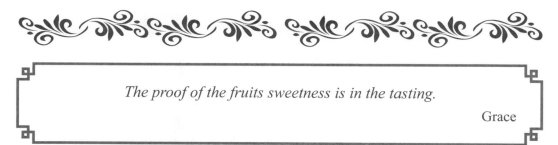

The proof of the fruits sweetness is in the tasting.

Grace

South Kona Fruit Stand Smoothie Blend
2 servings

2 C frozen fruit chunks, apple banana, strawberry papaya, white sapote, mango or mamay

2 C juice, pineapple-coconut, apple or mango-peach

2 T macadamia nut butter or 10 cashews soaked 2 hours

2 tsp bee pollen

1 tsp Kona grown spirulina

2 T hemp or rice protein powder

A great way to start the day, or a delicious snack after swimming at one of the bays. Stop by this delightful South Kona stand for a great gourmet selection of organic exotic fruit and a tropical smoothie made to order!

The diet which serves us best will be one which produces health and limits disease, is capable of being grown and produced by natural methods, and produces enough food for all the people of the world.

Bill Tara, quoted in *Compassion for All Creatures,* Janice Gray Kolb

 # Salads

Asian Salad
4+ servings

1 small head Napa cabbage
4 oz pkg. mung bean sprouts
2 medium carrots, grated large
2 tsp Thai Kitchen spicy red chili sauce
2 T sesame oil
Juice of 1 lemon
1 T rice vinegar
1 T tamari
½ C Gomasio (p. 80)

Thin chop leafy green part of cabbage (save base portion for stir fry or soup).

Toss together remaining ingredients and let meld, tossing again a few times.

Salad will significantly shrink.

Garnish with Gomasio.

> *I was learning that the same food choices that do so much to prevent disease—that give you the most vitality, the strongest immune system, and the greatest life expectancy—were also the ones that took the least toll on the environment, conserved our precious natural resources, and were the most compassionate toward our fellow creatures.*
>
> John Robbins, *The Food Revolution*

Beet Salad
4 servings

8 medium beets (2-3 inch)
¼ C apple cider vinegar
1 T agave nectar
2 cloves garlic, minced
¼ C red onion, minced
1 medium cucumber, peeled & minced
1 T fresh dill, finely chopped
1 tsp caraway seeds
½ tsp pepper
1 tsp crystal salt

Peel beets and cut into ½" slices.

Steam until just tender (approximately 15 minutes), then let cool.

Mix remaining ingredients together and let stand for 10 minutes.

Add cooled beets and chill well.

A dollop of Tofu Sour Cream (p. 83) will enhance both flavor and color.

Cabbage Salad with Arame
6 + servings

2 C Napa or purple cabbage,
 thinly shredded
1 C grated carrots,
½ C roasted almonds, chopped
1 green apple, in small chunks
1 C Arame seaweed, soaked 20
 minutes, then drained
½ C green onion, diced
2 T cilantro, minced
4 tsp pickled ginger, chopped
½ avocado in chunks

Dressing:
 ½ C water
 ¼ C lemon juice
 4 T tahini raw
 1 T tamari
 black pepper to taste

Whisk dressing ingredients together in a bowl and pour over salad veggies.

Combine above ingredients in a bowl.

Sweet and Sour Dressing (p. 77) also accentuates this salad superlatively.
Allow dressing to meld in salad for 1/2 hour remixing occasionally.

Chopped Vegetable Avocado Salad

2 servings

⅛ white cabbage, shredded
2 stalks celery, chopped
¼ red bell pepper chopped
8 med dinosaur kale leaves, finely
    chopped
⅛ red onion, finely chopped
¼ beet, finely grated
½ med avocado pulp, mashed

1 lemon, juiced
2 cloves garlic, finely grated
½ tsp crystal salt
1 T sesame oil
2 tsp agave nectar
2 tsp mixed fresh herbs (rosemary,
    thyme, sage...) finely chopped

Mix together well. Add some hot red pepper for added zest!
Garnish with Dulse seaweed

Cole Slaw

6 servings

4 C cabbage, grated or shredded
2 medium carrots, grated
½ C Vegenaise
2 T lemon juice
½ red onion, finely chopped

½ tsp crystal salt
⅛ tsp black pepper
1 T poppy seeds
2 tsp agave nectar

Mix all ingredients together.
Refrigerate for several hours to allow flavors to blend.

> *A diet of whole natural foods not only promoted the reversal of heart disease, but also provides the body with a rich and continuous supply of phyto-chemicals, nutrient like substances that fight cancer formation. These helpful chemicals are not found in any animal products...*
>
> Douglas J. Lilie, Ph.D. & Alan Goldhammer, D.C., *The Pleasure Trap*

Cranberry Apple Walnut Salad
6 servings

3–4 apples, Fuji, Gala or Yellow
   Delicious, diced medium
3 stalks celery, sliced thin
½ C fresh cranberries, chopped
   small or seedless grapes cut in half
1 C crushed pineapple, drained
½ C walnuts, soaked 12 hours
   chopped large
⅓ C Vegenaise
¼ C fresh lemon juice (about 2
   lemons)
1 tsp crystal salt

Put all the ingredients in a salad bowl and stir together.

For an artful presentation, serve in large leaves of lettuce on chilled salad plates.

> *Not that long ago, people who ate food that was healthy, environmentally friendly, and caused no animals to suffer were considered health nuts, while those who ate food that caused disease, took a staggering toll on the resource base, and depended on immense animal suffering were considered normal. But all this is changing.*
>
> John Robbins, *The Food Revolution*

Cucumber Zucchini Salad
A light and refreshing salad; a great accompaniment to raw food meals.
4 servings

1 medium cucumber, grated
1 medium zucchini, grated
2 or 3 T fresh cilantro,
    finely chopped

Dressing
¼ C olive oil
⅛ C lemon juice or apple cider vinegar
2 cloves garlic, pressed
1 T Tamari

Combine cucumber, zucchini and cilantro.

A great way to chop cilantro and other fresh herbs is to first remove large stems then chop with scissors in a small bowl.

Blend dressing ingredients together and pour over salad.

Greek Salad
6 servings

½ lb Romaine lettuce, shredded
½ lb spinach, lightly chopped
½ C almonds, soaked and peeled
1 cucumber, peeled and sliced

½ small red onion, thinly sliced
1 can Santa Cruz green olives, drained
    and cut in half
2 tomatoes, cut in eighths.

Mix in a bowl and serve with Greek Dressing (p. 74).

Green Papaya Carrot Salad
2 servings

1 green papaya
¼ red onion, minced
2 carrots, peeled and grated
2 T cilantro, minced
1" ginger, finely grated
½ red pepper cut in thin strips
½ C white cabbage, finely shredded
1 tomato, chopped
¼ C lime juice
2 T toasted sesame oil
1 T tamari or ume vinegar
⅛ tsp red pepper flakes
½ tsp coriander powder
1 T agave

Choose a green papaya with a yellow spot starting. Peel & grate papaya.

Combine vegetables in a bowl.

Mix dressing ingredients together.

Pour over salad.

Enjoy!

Jia's Waldorf Salad
6 servings

2 C cabbage, finely shredded
4 stalks celery, chopped
2 apples, cut in small chunks
½ C walnuts, in small pieces
½ C raisins
1 orange, juiced

⅓ C tahini
2 T white miso
1 T ginger juice
1 T lemon juice

Opt: 1 T honey

Mix dressing ingredients together then blend with salad.
Refrigerate for several hours, stirring occasionally to allow flavors to meld.

Kale Salad with Lemon Flax Dressing
4 servings

1 bunch kale, any variety, de-stemmed and finely chopped
2 medium tomatoes, diced small
1 large cucumber, diced small
1 medium avocado, diced small
2 tsp minced red onion
¼ C flax, hemp or olive oil
¼ C brown rice vinegar or lemon juice
1 T tamari
Opt: 2 tsp dulse flakes

In a salad bowl, put all the ingredients, except the avocado, and toss to mix. Just before serving add the avocado.

This salad can be served soon after it is made or cover and set in the refrigerator for several hours to marinate.

Health is best supported by the removal of all meat, fish, fowl, eggs. dairy products, and added oil, salt, sugar, and refined carbohydrates. Also to be avoided are recreational drugs such as alcohol, caffeine, and tobacco. Health is most effectively promoted by healthful living—consuming a diet of whole natural foods, exercising, getting appropriate rest, and avoiding toxic substances. Such a lifestyle not only prevents disease, but in many cases, is able to reverse disease and help restore health and well-being.''

Douglas L. Lislie, Ph.D., Alan Goldhamer, D.C., *The Pleasure Trap*

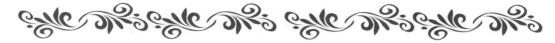

Lemon Dill Beets and Greens
2 servings

4 medium beets and their greens
¼ C pine nuts
3 T olive oil
3 T fresh lemon juice
¼ tsp crystal salt
¼ C finely chopped fresh dill weed

Cut the greens off the beets. Cut the beets in quarters or smaller. Remove the stems from the greens and cut the greens in ribbons.

In a large pot with a steamer basket, put 1-inch of water. Cover and bring to a gentle boil. Put the beets in the steamer basket, cover and steam until just tender, around 8 to 12 minutes. Add the beet greens and continue to steam until the greens are wilted, about 2 more minutes.

In a blender, put the pine nuts, olive oil, lemon juice and crystal salt. Blend until smooth and creamy. If needed, add a tablespoon or 2 of water so the mixture flows freely through the blender blades.

In a large bowl, put the steamed beets and greens. Pour the blended pine nut dressing over the top and sprinkle with the dill weed.

Serve this salad warm or chill first.

Keep in a covered glass container in the refrigerator for up to 3 days.

Mandala Garden Salad
4 servings

½ lb Romaine lettuce, torn or chopped
¼ lb gourmet salad mix
2 carrots, peeled and grated
½ beet, peeled and grated
⅛ red cabbage, finely chopped
1 Asian cucumber, thinly cut in rounds
2 oz clover sprouts
2 oz sunflower sprouts
1 tomato, sliced
½ red onion, in rings or thinly sliced
½ avocado, in chunks

Optional:
  jicama, sweet red peppers, celery,
  toasted or soaked seeds
  and nuts, dulse, edible flowers.

In a large salad bowl, combine lettuce, salad mix and ½ rest of ingredients except beet, tomatoes, onion and avocado.

Use remaining ingredients to decorate the top of salad.

Suns, hearts, and spirals, are all beautiful mandala creations.

> *The concept of lokahi gives us one of the most fundamental principles of the Hawaii Diet. It points out that if we are to be as healthy, or as whole, as possible, then the food we eat should also be as whole as possible.*
> Dr. Terry Shintani, M.D., J.D., M.P.H., "The Hawaii Diet"

Quinoa Salad

8 servings

2 C quinoa, rinsed thoroughly
3 ½ C water
2 carrots, peeled and finely chopped
3 celery stalks, finely chopped
¼ red onion, finely chopped
½ red pepper, diced in small pieces
2 T tamari
3 T olive oil
1 lemon, juiced
2 cloves garlic, finely grated
2 T chopped parsley
¼ C almonds, roasted & chopped
1 can green olives, chopped

Bring water to a boil in a 2-quart pot, covered.

Add quinoa, return to boil, lower heat, cover, and simmer for 20 minutes.

Turn off heat and immediately transfer grains to a bowl.

Let quinoa cool and add remaining ingredients.

Dress with Miso Magic (p. 76) or leave as is.

When the five senses and the mind are still, and reason itself rests in silence, then begins the Path Supreme. This calm steadiness of the senses is called Yoga.

The Upanishads, translated by Joan Mascaro

Raw Kale Salad
4 servings

½ lb kale, younger leaves
½ lb Romaine lettuce
½ C olive oil
1 T tamari
¼ C fresh lemon juice
½ red onion, chopped
2 cloves garlic, minced
1 C raw sunflower seeds,
  soaked 2 hours and drained

Cut kale & lettuce into finely chopped strips.

Add remaining ingredients and thoroughly massage together to release vegetable juices.

Let marinate for at least half an hour, stirring occasionally.

Garnish with soaked sunflower seeds.

Soba Salad
4 servings

1 - 8 oz pkg. soba (buckwheat) noodles
1 medium avocado, mashed
8 sun dried tomatoes
1 red pepper, finely chopped
1 T Italian seasoning
2 medium tomatoes, finely chopped
1 T tamari
2 cloves garlic, pressed

Cook drain, and cool soba noodles.

Soak sun dried tomatoes in water or olive oil for at least ½ hour and then chop.

Mix all ingredients together in a bowl and serve.

There is one ruler, the Spirit that is in all things, who transforms his own form into many. Only the wise who see him in their souls attain the eternal joy.

The Upanishads, translated by Juan Mascaro

Sunny Summer Salad
4–6 servings

¼ C raw sunflower seeds
1 tsp tamari
cayenne pepper, to taste

2 medium tomatoes, diced large
1 avocado, diced large
1 red or yellow bell pepper,
   diced small
1 small cucumber, diced small
¼ pound shiitake mushrooms,
   sliced thin (about 1 C)
½ C coarsely cut fresh basil leaves
¼ C coarsely cut dulse (sea vegetable)
3 T olive oil
3 T fresh lemon juice
1 T finely chopped red onion
¼ tsp crystal salt

Heat a small dry frying pan, over medium high heat. Add the sunflower seeds and lightly toast, stirring often, until a light golden color, about 4 minutes. Remove from heat, add the tamari and cayenne and stir well. Set aside.

In a medium salad bowl, put the remaining ingredients and stir to mix. Sprinkle the toasted sunflower seeds over the top.

For an artful presentation, serve on large leaves of lettuce on chilled salad plates.

And when a man sees that the God in himself is the same God in all that is, he hurts not himself by hurting others: then he goes indeed to the highest path.

The Upanishads, translated by Juan Mascaro

Traditional Potato Salad

8 servings

2 lbs boiling potatoes,
   peeled and chopped
2 medium carrots, peeled
3 celery stalks
⅓ red onion
1 small red bell pepper
1 C frozen peas, thawed
½ lb green beans, cooked and chopped
   in fourths
¾ C Vegenaise
1½ T Dijon mustard
¼ C fresh lemon juice
2 cloves garlic, pressed
¼ C fresh parsley, chopped
¼ C fresh dill, minced
2 tsp crystal salt

In a large pot, cover potatoes with salted water and boil until tender, about 12 minutes.
When done, rinse and cool under cold water.
Let stand until completely cool.
Finely chop carrots, celery, onion and pepper.
Add veggies to potatoes.
Mix dressing ingredients together and pour over vegetables and potatoes and toss. Chill.
Opt: For a flavorful addition add ½ C sliced olives.
Sweet potatoes and yams may also be used to replace some of the potatoes.

Tempeh Salad or Main Course

4 servings

1 block cooked tempeh (p. 140)
½ C Vegenaise
1 carrot, grated
2 stalks celery, finely chopped
¼ red onion, finely chopped
2 cloves garlic, minced
1 T tamari

1 T lemon juice
2 T fresh herbs, chopped (basil,
   cilantro and parsley)
½ tsp pepper
Opt: 2 tsp curry powder
   and or 1 T Dijon mustard

Break tempeh into bite size pieces and mix with remaining ingredients.
For a hot dish lightly sauté vegetables & spices and add Vegenaise at end.

Tempeh Thai Vegetable Salad
4 servings

Marinated Tempeh
½ pound tempeh
2 T tamari
1 T finely grated fresh ginger
2 cloves garlic, finely grated or pressed
2 T coconut oil

Salad
1 Napa cabbage, finely shredded
  (4 cups)
1 large tomato, diced small
1 medium carrot, grated large
1 small diakon, grated large
1 C mung bean sprouts

Thai Vinaigrette
¼ C fresh lime or lemon juice
2 T toasted sesame oil
2 T sesame or grape seed oil
2 T tamari
2 T agave nectar or other sweetener
1 tsp curry powder
½ C coarsely chopped fresh mint leaves

Garnishes
½ C raw jungle peanuts, coarsely
  chopped
¼ C shredded dried coconut,
  unsweetened

Marinated Tempeh: Cut the tempeh in half horizontally then cut in ½-inch pieces. In a quart jar , put the tempeh and all the ingredients for the Marinated Tempeh, except the coconut oil. Let sit for 1 hour or up to 12 hours in the refrigerator. Turn the jar several time to coat the tempeh.

In a medium frying pan, slowly heat the coconut oil. Add the Marinated Tempeh and cook until a golden color on both sides, about 8 minutes.

Salad: In a large salad bowl, put all the ingredients for the salad.

Thai Vinaigrette: In a small bowl, put all the ingredients for vinaigrette and stir together.

Garnishes: Heat a small dry frying pan over medium high heat. Add the peanuts and toast them, stirring frequently, until they are lightly toasted, about 5 minutes. Put the toasted peanuts in a blender and pulse to chop coarsely. Heat the same dry frying pan. Add the coconut and toast, stirring frequently, until it is a golden color, about 4 minutes.

Add the Marinated Tempeh to the Salad and pour the Thai Vinaigrette over all and toss to mix. Sprinkle the toasted peanuts and coconut over the top.

Zucchini Salad

4 servings

4 medium zucchinis, grated (about 2 pounds)	Grate zucchini into a bowl.
2 T vinegar, balsamic or brown rice	Mix dressing ingredients together and pour over zucchini.
2 T olive oil	
1 T Dijon mustard	
8 basil leaves, thinly sliced	Garnish with chopped parsley.
½ tsp spike	
¼ tsp pepper	Variation: half of the zucchini may be substituted with cucumber.
2 T parsley, chopped	

O, Heavenly Father,
We thank Thee for food, and remember the hungry.
We thank Thee for health, and remember the sick.
We thank Thee for friends, and remember the friendless.
We thank Thee for freedom, and remember the enslaved.
May these remembrances stir us to service,
That Thy gifts to us may be used for others. Amen.

Abigail van Buren

 # Dressings

Here are a wide variety of delicious, easy to prepare dressings.
Simply blend all ingredients. Note: 4 T (¼ C) provides 2-3 servings.

Almond Caesar Dressing

12 almonds, roasted
3 garlic cloves, minced
2 T Dijon mustard
2 T nutritional yeast
2 T tamari

2 T tahini
4 T lemon juice
½ C water
4 T olive oil

Creamy Onion Dressing

½ C olive oil
½ C Original Rice Dream
4 stalks green onion leaves
12 almonds, soaked
1 T raw apple cider vinegar

2 T lime or lemon juice
1 tsp crystal salt
1 T fresh parsley, chopped
1 tsp Bernard Jensen's Broth or Spike
Opt: 1 T sweetener

The American fast-food diet and the meat-eating habits of the wealthy around the world support a world food system that diverts food resources from the hungry. A diet higher in whole grains and legumes and lower in beef and other meat is not just healthier for ourselves but also contributes to changing the world system that feeds some people and leaves others hungry.

Dr. Walden Bello, Executive Director,
Institute for Food and Development Policy

French Dressing

¼ C apple cider vinegar
¾ C olive oil
2 T honey
1 tomato
2 T fresh basil, chopped

2 T fresh parsley, chopped
1 T Dijon mustard
2 cloves garlic, minced
1 T tamari

Greek Dressing

½ C olive oil
4 T water
2 cloves garlic, chopped
2 tsp Dijon mustard
1 T tamari
1 lemon, juiced

1 T Balsamic vinegar
1 T Sucanat
2 tomatoes, chopped
½ avocado
Handful of parsley
1 T fresh thyme, minced

Green Raw Goddess Creamy Dressing

1 small ripe avocado
2 C Awesome Sesame Mylk (p. 49)
Soak juice from ½ C Gogi berries
   soaked in 1 C water 2 hrs (½ C)
¼ C fresh lemon juice
4 cloves garlic, minced

2 T white miso (Westbrae) or
   1 tsp crystal salt
¼ C fresh cilantro, chopped
1 tsp fresh thyme, chopped
⅛ tsp cayenne or jalapeño pepper
Opt: 1 T nutritional yeast

Raw-some dressing, add soaked gogis to your salad!

Herb Dressing

½ C olive oil
2 cloves garlic, minced
2 T maple syrup
4 T apple cider vinegar

1 tsp Dijon mustard
1 tsp fresh dill
1 tsp fresh parsley
½ tsp crystal salt

Italian Dressing

¾ C sun dried tomatoes soaked in
   ¾ C olive oil for 10 minutes
2 T balsamic vinegar
2 T lemon juice
1 T maple syrup
1 T fresh thyme, minced

1 T Dijon mustard
2 cloves garlic, minced
1 T fresh parsley, minced
½ C water
crystal salt to taste

Lemon Tahini Dressing

½ C raw tahini
½ C water
¼ C olive oil
¼ C fresh lemon juice
¼ C chopped parsley leaves
1 T poppy seeds

2 T tamari or white miso
1 tsp cumin
2 dates, pits removed or
1 T raw (Lehua) honey
2 cloves garlic, crushed

Miso Magic Dressing

A wild combination of all our favorite healthy ingredients in one great dressing!

½ ripe avocado
2 tsp apple cider vinegar
1 T lemon juice
¼ C safflower oil
1 C Eden Soy rice mylk
½ C Vegenaise

2 T Westbrae white miso
2 T nutritional yeast
1 T agave nectar
¼ C fresh cilantro or basil, minced
2 cloves garlic, minced
¼ tsp jalapeno pepper powder

Papaya Noni Dressing

1 medium papaya, pulp only
½ medium avocado
¼ C fresh noni juice
1 tsp crystal salt
1 T raw honey

2 T lemon or lime juice
1 T grated ginger
½ tsp pepper
2 T fresh parsley
Opt 1 tsp fresh mint

Papaya Seed Tarragon Dressing

A light and zesty addition to many dishes.

½ C safflower oil
¼ C soy rice mylk (Eden)
2 T brown rice vinegar
2 T lime juice
2 T fresh papaya seeds
2 T nutritional yeast

1 T fresh parsley, chopped
1 T fresh tarragon, chopped
1 T agave nectar
2 cloves garlic, minced
½ tsp coriander powder

Simply Excellent Dressing

Place these ingredients directly on your garden salad, amounts to taste.

High Lignin flax oil
Umeboshi vinegar
lemon wedges
fresh herbs of choice

nutritional yeast
dulse leaves
tamari or crystal salt
black or red pepper

Sun-Dried Tomato Balsamic Vinaigrette

½ C olive oil
¼ C balsamic vinegar
¼ C fresh lemon juice
2–4 sun-dried tomatoes

1 clove garlic, crushed
1 T finely chopped basil
1 T agave nectar
½ tsp crystal salt

Sweet & Sour Dressing

Excellent on salads as well as with protein dishes

¾ C grape seed oil
¼ C water
¼ C fresh lemon juice
¼ C raw apple cider vinegar
2 T nutritional yeast
4-6 dates, pits removed

2 T tamari
2 tsp curry powder
1 T Dijon mustard
1 T finely chopped cilantro
1 T finely grated fresh ginger

Thai Dressing

2 T fresh ginger, finely grated
2 T raw apple cider vinegar
½ C water
½ C safflower oil
2 T brown rice miso
2 T tahini

2 T sesame oil
⅔ C green onion, chopped
1 T maple syrup
4 T lime juice
1 T basil or cilantro
Dash of jalapeno or cayenne pepper

Tofu Dill Salad Dressing

½ lb soft tofu, crumbled
¼ C olive oil
¼ C lemon juice
¼ C water or more as needed
1 T fresh dill weed

1 T agave nectar
2 T tamari
2 cloves garlic, crushed
1 T nutritional yeast
Opt: ½ tsp black pepper

Vitality Dressing

1 ¼ C olive oil
⅛ C tamari
2 tsp coriander powder
1 T fresh ginger, minced
1 T cumin powder
½ C fresh basil, chopped

1 T prepared mustard
¼ tsp pepper
2 lemons, juiced
Opt: 1 tsp dill weed
    2 tsp onion powder

This delicious dressing is good on everything, including salads!

 # Condiments

Apricot Apple Chutney
8+ servings

1 T sesame oil
1 small yellow onion, diced small
½ small jalapeño pepper, with seeds
   removed and some white ribs left
   for hotness
½ tsp cumin seeds
1 C unfiltered apple juice
½ C dried apricots or 1 C fresh,
   cut small

½ C currants or raisins
2 green apples, cored and diced large
1 T finely grated fresh ginger
½ tsp cinnamon powder
½ tsp cardamom powder
¼ tsp crystal salt
¼ C agave nectar or other sweetener
2 T fresh lemon juice

In a large sauce pan, heat the oil. Add the onion, jalapeno pepper, and cumin seeds and sauté 3 minutes. Add the remaining ingredients, cover and simmer until the apples are very tender, about 20 minutes. Remove the lid and continue to simmer until thick, about 5 minutes. Serve at room temperature or chilled.

Cucumber Raita
4 servings

Salad
2 medium cucumbers, sliced thin
1 medium carrot, grated large

Dressing
2 T raw tahini (sesame butter)
2 T rice vinegar or fresh lemon juice
2 T water
½ tsp cumin powder
½ tsp toasted cumin seeds
½ tsp crystal salt
pinch of cayenne

Salad: In a small salad bowl, put the cucumbers and carrot.

Dressing: In a small bowl, put all the ingredients for the dressing and whisk together.

Pour the dressing over the salad and toss to mix. Chill for ½ hour before serving.

Gomasio
8–12 servings

1 C brown unhulled sesame seeds
2 tsp crystal salt

In a heavy skillet on medium high heat roast sesame seeds with salt until seeds are golden brown. Grind ½ mixture.

Green Olive Tapenade
about 10 servings

2 T extra virgin olive oil
2 onions, thinly sliced and chopped
4 cloves garlic, minced

1 can pitted green olives, chopped
2 stalks celery, finely chopped
½ red bell pepper, finely chopped
1 T fresh thyme, finely chopped
1 T Dijon mustard
¼ tsp cayenne pepper
1 tsp crystal salt
1 T lemon juice

Sauté onions and garlic in oil on medium high heat until onions are translucent (5 minutes).

Add remaining ingredients and sauté for one more minute and then lightly blend mixture in a food processor to the consistency of salsa.

> *The ecological and social crises we face are inflamed by an economic system dependent on accelerating growth. This self-destructing political economy sets its goals and measures its performance in terms of ever-increasing corporate profits—in other words by how fast materials can be extracted from Earth and turned into consumer products, weapons, and waste.*
>
> www.Joannamacy.net

Mango-Apple Chutney

2 T grape seed or coconut oil
1 tsp cinnamon, ground
½ tsp coriander powder
½ tsp allspice
⅛ tsp clove powder
2 T ginger, minced
½ tsp crystal salt

1 T lemon juice
2 T apple cider vinegar
1 C fresh mango, chopped
2 C fresh apple, grated
2 T agave nectar or maple syrup
½ C raisins
¼ C apple juice

Heat oil in a sauce pan over medium high heat, add spices and sauté for 2 minutes. Add remaining ingredients including apple juice, bring to a low boil then simmer for 20 minutes (until liquid is reduced).

Great on many dishes! This chutney will keep one week in the fridge.

Raw Fig Chutney

makes ½ cups

2 T minced fresh ginger
½ C flaked coconut
½ C fresh cilantro or mint
½ C figs

1 green apple, grated
1 tsp cinnamon
½ tsp allspice
1 T fresh lemon juice
pinch of crystal salt

Pulse all ingredients to a paste in a food processor.

The only way to live is to live and let live.

Mahatma K Gandhi, quoted in
Compassion for All Creatures, Janice Gray Kolb

Roasted Seeds & Nuts

1 C nuts or seeds of choice:
   almonds, cashews, sunflower,
   pumpkin, macadamia nut, etc.
2 T tamari or 1 T umeboshi
   vinegar
Opt: 1 T raw coconut oil

Roast nuts or seeds over medium
high heat in a stainless or cast iron
pan for 3 to 5 minutes, while stirring
until golden brown or bake in an oven
at 350° for about 7 minutes stirring
occasionally.

Turn off heat, and add liquid, stirring constantly to mix well.
Let cool before serving.

Raw Tapenade
8 servings

1 C olives. deseeded and chopped
½ C walnuts, soaked and chopped
2 garlic cloves, pressed
2 stalks green onion leafy part,
   chopped

1 T lemon juice
1 T olive oil
1 T fresh parsley, chopped
2 tsp fresh thyme, chopped
1 tsp crystal salt

Mix together in a bowl.

Raw Tomato Ketchup
8+ servings

⅔ C sun dried tomatoes,
   soaked ½ hour in warm water
4 medium tomatoes, chopped
3 pitted dates

2 T apple cider vinegar
1 ½ tsp crystal salt
Dash of pepper

Mix all ingredients together in a food processor.
Ketchup will store well in the refrigerator.

Super Spice

1 T caraway seeds, rough ground	1 tsp cardamom powder
1 T coriander powder	½ tsp nutmeg powder
3 bay leaves, finely ground	½ tsp anise powder
1 T cinnamon powder	1 tsp crystal salt
1 T ginger powder	¼ tsp clove powder

Mix spices well and store in a tightly sealed jar.
A gourmet condiment for many dishes!

Tofu Mayonnaise
8 servings

1 C soft tofu	1 T agave nectar
4 tsp Ume vinegar	4 T grape seed oil
¼ C lemon juice	Opt: ½ tsp coriander powder
1 T Dijon mustard	

Blend all ingredients to a creamy consistency.
This is a deliciously cost effective mayonnaise recipe.

Tofu Sour Cream
12 servings

2¼ C tofu, silken or medium	3 T lemon juice
½ C safflower or grape seed oil	4 cloves garlic, crushed
4 tsp Tamari	2 T parsley, chopped
1½ T maple syrup	½ tsp pepper

Blend all ingredients in a food processor until creamy. Add parsley and lightly
pulse so parsley is well mixed without turning the cream green.
Excellent with potato dishes as well as on raw or cooked vegetables.

Yellow Tomato Salsa
Makes 3 cups

2 large yellow tomatoes, cut in quarters
1 medium yellow bell pepper, seeds and ribs removed, cut large
1 small jalapeño pepper, leaving some of the ribs and seeds for heat
3 green onions, white part only, cut in large pieces
1 C fresh cilantro leaves
2 T fresh lime or lemon juice
½ tsp crystal salt

Put all the ingredients in a food processor, with the S-shaped blade.
Using the pulse switch, coarsely chop the ingredients.

Protecting something as wide as this planet is still an abstraction for many. Yet I see the day in our own lifetime that reverence for the natural systems—the oceans, the rainforests, the soil, the grasslands, and all other living things—will be so strong that no narrow ideology based upon politics or economics will overcome it.

Jerry Brown, Governor of California, www.Joannamacy.net

 # Dips

Carrot Almond Pâté
8 servings
This recipe requires the use of a Champion Juicer.

1 C almonds   1 lb (6-8) carrots   1 T tamari

Soak almonds overnight, then remove skins. Peel, top and tail carrots.

Attach homogenizer blank to Champion Juicer and process a handful of nuts with each carrot. Run food through twice for a smoother consistency.

Add tamari and serve as a pâté with sprouted Mana Bread or celery sticks.

For a decorative treat shape pâté into a heart and ring with grated beets.

Hummus
8+ servings

2 cans garbanzo beans,
  drained (Eden preferred)
4 cloves garlic, chopped
6 T olive oil
6 T tahini
2 lemons, juiced
2 tsp cumin
2 T tamari
handful of parsley, chopped

Add garbanzo beans, garlic and all other ingredients except parsley to food processor and blend to a creamy consistency.
Add parsley at the end and fine chop by gently pulsing.
Adjust flavor to taste.
A dash of cayenne pepper may be added for heat.

> *I am in favor of animal rights as well as human rights. That is the way of a whole human being.*
>
> Abraham Lincoln, quoted in
> *Compassion for All Creatures,* Janice Gray Kolb

Carrot Cashew Dip
8 servings

4 medium carrots, peeled
3 C raw cashew pieces (soaked 1 hour)
   or 1 lb mac nuts (soaked 4-8 hours)
2 cloves garlic, minced
4 T coconut or sunflower oil
   or ½ of a small avocado
2 T tamari
1 T lemon juice
¼ tsp jalapeno powder
⅓ C water

2 T red onion, finely chopped
¼ C celery, finely chopped
2 T parsley, finely chopped
¼ tsp paprika

Chop carrots into big chunks, place in a food processor and blend thoroughly.

Mix remaining ingredients in slowly, scraping sides occasionally with a rubber spatula.

If using mac nuts, thoroughly process them separately first, then process carrots, and add blended mac nuts with the other ingredients except onion, celery, parsley, and paprika

Blend until creamy and transfer to a bowl.

Mix remaining ingredients into dip and sprinkle paprika on top.

People are now neuroadapted to a diet that is overly rich in animal-based and unhealthful processed foods. The human, economic, and environmental cost of this situation is staggering. We are a civilization ensnared in a dietary pleasure trap. Modern foods are like magical poisons, hyper-stimulating the brain's pleasure centers, while simultaneously destroying health.

Douglas L. Lislie, Ph.D., Alan Goldhamer, D.C., *The Pleasure Trap*

Guacamole
8+ servings

3 medium avocados
2 cloves garlic, pressed
2 tsp crystal salt
2 tomatoes, chopped
1 lemon, juiced
Handful of cilantro, chopped
dash cayenne pepper
½ small red onion, chopped

Mash avocados.

Add all ingredients. Mix together.

Check flavor.

Serve with chips and garnishes.

Opt: add ¼ C of a favorite salsa

Mexican Black Bean Dip
6 servings

2 -15-ounce cans organic black beans,
   drained or 1 cup dried black beans
   cooked to very tender
4 green onions with tops, sliced thin
2 medium red or yellow tomatoes,
   diced small
1 Anaheim chili, diced small
1 avocado, diced small

½ C fresh cilantro leaves,
   coarsely chopped
¼ C fresh lemon juice
2 T tamari
2 cloves garlic, grated small or pressed
1 tsp taco seasoning powder
cayenne pepper, to taste

In a large bowl, put the canned or cooked beans and mash slightly. Add the remaining ingredients and stir together. Serve with baked corn chips.

Shiva's Super Dip

8+ servings

2 C almonds, soaked
¼ C chopped cilantro
¼ C chopped parsley
2 stalks celery, finely chopped
⅛ red onion, finely chopped
1 beet, grated

2 T lemon juice
1 tsp coriander powder
1 tsp cumin powder
½ tsp curry powder
½ tsp red chili powder
1 tsp crystal salt

Process almonds in food processor to a smooth consistency. In a bowl mix all ingredients together. place on a serving tray in desired shape, and decorate with tomatoes and grated carrot.

ॐ नमः शिवाय

OM Namah Shivaya
I bow to whatever Good is happening and to Whomsoever is doing it.
Said to be the oldest mantra.

www. Babaji.net, devoted to Truth, Simplicity, and Love

Sunny Almond Spread
8 servings

1 C raw almonds, soaked 8 to 12 hours

1 C raw sunflower seeds,
   soaked 4 hours

¼ C fresh lemon juice

2 T tamari

2 cloves garlic, crushed

1 medium carrot, grated small

½ C finely chopped parsley leaves

In a food processor, with the S-shaped blade, put the soaked almonds and sunflower seeds, lemon juice, tamari and garlic and process until smooth. If needed, add a little water, a tablespoon at a time, so the mixture flows freely through the blade. This spread is best when thick, so not too much water. Stop the food processor, add the grated carrot and chopped parsley and stir to mix. Serve with slices of carrot and celery. See the photos on the back cover and inside front cover for ideas on how to present this spread.

Dare to Vision

Out of this darkness a new world can arise, not to be constructed by our minds so much as to emerge from our dreams. Even though we cannot see clearly how it's going to turn out, we are still called to let the future into our imagination. We will never be able to build what we have not first cherished in our hearts.

www.Joannamacy.net

Sunny Dip
8 servings

2 C sunflower seeds, soaked 2 hours.
¼ C lemon juice
⅛ C apple cider vinegar
2 T tamari or white miso
¼ C basil leaves, packed
1 T agave nectar
2 stalks celery, chopped
⅛ tsp cayenne pepper

Drain Sunflower seeds and add to a food processor.

Add rest of ingredients and process.

It may be necessary to open and scrape sides of processor or add more water to achieve desired consistency.

A tantalizing dip for crackers or vegetable slices

There are forces at work in our culture that tell us we are separate from life. But there are forces at work in our hearts that are helping us to awaken, and take our place on this Earth in harmony with the other beings who draw breath from the same source as we do We are not here to abuse and exploit other creatures. We are here to live and help live. Every meal is part of the journey.

John Robbins, *The Food Revolution*

 # Sauces

Almond Pesto Sauce
8-12 servings

2 C fresh basil leaves, chopped
2 C raw almonds soaked 12-24 hours
½ C olive oil
2 heaping T white miso

4 cloves fresh garlic, pressed
1 T lemon juice
pinch of cayenne pepper
Water for desired consistency

Blend all ingredients in a food processor.
Add more water if a smoother consistency is desired.
This sauce is full of live enzymes and will last for 2-3 days in the fridge.

Bliss Sauce
4–6 servings

½ C cashews, lightly roasted
½ tsp ground coriander
¼ tsp nutmeg
¼ tsp turmeric
1 C water

1 tsp agave nectar
1 T white miso
1 T coconut oil
1 T lime juice
1 T parsley, minced

Blend all ingredients together except parsley which is mixed in after.

Nothing will benefit human health and increase chances for survival of life on Earth as much as the evolution to a vegetarian diet.

Albert Einstein

Erin's Island Magic Sauce
6-8 servings

1 T coconut oil
4-5 large cloves of garlic, minced
½ red onion, minced fine
1 T freshly grated ginger
¼ tsp freshly grated turmeric root
 (olena) or ½ tsp turmeric powder
½ tsp curry powder
1 T cumin powder (freshly ground if
 possible)

Crystal salt or tamari, to taste or a bit
 of both
1 T white miso
2 T almond butter
2 T tahini
1 C of water, or coconut water
1 tsp agave nectar
1½ T nutritional yeast

Saute garlic, onions, ginger, turmeric, curry powder, cumin powder in the coconut oil. Reduce heat and add the miso, almond butter, tahini, honey and water or coconut water. Simmer a bit then add the nutritional yeast and salt. Let simmer on low for a few more minutes until thick and creamy. Garnish with chopped cilantro or basil. A magical addition as a topping on steamed veggies and rice etc.

Gombu Sauce
8 servings

2½ C water
2-3" x 8" strips Kombu sea weed
½ C dried Shitaki mushrooms
1 C Gomasio, made with ½ the salt
 (p. 80)

In a small pot bring water to boil and simmer Kombu and mushrooms for 20 minutes.
Cool, remove Kombu and mushrooms and blend stock water with salt-decreased Gomasio.

Excellent with Buddha Balls (p. 129) or as a base for dressings.
Other added ingredients may be experimented with, like fresh lime juice,
Thai Kitchen spicy red chili sauce or agave nectar.

Indonesian Almond Butter Sauce
6–8 servings

¾ C roasted almond butter
4 cloves garlic, peeled
1 inch ginger, thinly sliced
4 T tamari
2 T Sucanat or rice syrup
½ tsp jalapeno pepper powder

2 T lime juice
2 T rice vinegar
2 T nutritional yeast
⅔ C water or veggie stock
2 T fresh cilantro, minced

Blend all ingredients, except cilantro, in a food processor until smooth.
Mix in most of the cilantro saving a little to spread over the surface of the sauce.
A tantalizing sauce to accent Thai dishes normally using peanut sauce
or may be used as an excellent exotic salad dressing.

Hot Thyme Sauce
8–10 servings

¾ C Vegenaise
6 T raw tahini
4 T white miso
2 T Balsamic vinegar
2 T agave nectar
2 T nutritional yeast
2 T Dijon mustard
1 T fresh thyme, finely chopped
¼ tsp cayenne pepper *or*
    1 T hot pepper sauce (to taste)
½ C rice mylk

Mix all ingredients together in a bowl.

Add more or less rice mylk depending on desired consistency.

For a delicious salad dressing, add double the rice mylk and 1 T lemon juice.

This sauce works wonders for vegetables and tofu. Unparalleled with Wild Rice Medley (p. 144)

Nirvana Sauce
8 servings

½ C raisins, soaked
1 C sun dried tomatoes, soaked
1 lemon, juiced
¼ C tahini

3 T white miso
2 stalks green onion, chopped
Handful of cilantro or basil, chopped
Pinch cayenne or jalapeno pepper

Lightly pulse in food processor

Orange Almond Sauce
8 servings

1 large orange, juiced
3 cloves garlic, chopped
½ C roasted almond butter
2 rounded T brown rice miso
2 T nutritional yeast
½" ginger, grated

Blend orange juice and garlic.
Add remaining ingredients and blend
thoroughly.
Exquisite on cooked and raw
vegetables!

Orange Ginger Marinade Sauce
4–6 servings

¼ C tamari
¼ C frozen orange juice concentrate
2 T fresh lemon juice
1 T agave nectar

1 T toasted or hot sesame oil
1 T finely grated fresh ginger
½ tsp finely grated orange rind
2 cloves garlic, grated small or pressed

In a quart jar, put all the ingredients, cover with the lid and shake well.
Use to marinate tofu and tempeh.

Peaceful Pesto Sauce
8 servings

2 C basil leaves, packed
3 T extra virgin olive oil
¼ C macadamia or pine nuts, raw
Juice of 1 lemon
4 cloves garlic, peeled & chopped

2 T white miso
3 T nutritional yeast
½ tsp pepper, fresh ground
⅛ C water

Add all ingredients to food processor and blend to desired consistency.

Secret Sauce
8–10 servings

1 C Vegenaise (grape seed oil variety)
4 T nutritional yeast
1 lemon, juiced
1 T Thai Kitchen Spicy Red Chili
    Sauce, or to taste
1 T toasted sesame oil
1 T raw agave nectar
1 T Ume vinegar
Handful cilantro, finely chopped

Combine all ingredients in a bowl.

Check flavor and adjust to desired taste.

Stir in cilantro.

Other herbs may be added, such as parsley and basil.

Shiitake Miso Gravy

8 servings

Flour Mixture
2 C water
¼ C white spelt flour or barley
   flour
1 T arrowroot powder

Miso Mixture
1 cup water
⅓ C brown rice miso
⅓ C nutritional yeast flakes

Sautéed Mushrooms
2 T grape seed oil or other
   vegetable oil
1 small yellow onion, diced small
½ pound shiitake mushrooms,
   sliced

Flour Mixture: In a medium bowl, put the 2 cups water, flour and arrowroot powder and whisk together until all lumps disappear. Set aside.

Miso Mixture: In a small bowl, put the 1 cup water, miso and nutritional yeast and whisk together. Set aside.

Sautéed Mushrooms: In a large frying pan, slowly heat the oil. Add the onion and sauté for 3 minutes. Add the mushrooms and sauté until tender, about 4 more minutes. Add the Flour Mixture and simmer, stirring often, until it begins to thicken, about 2 minutes. Add the Miso Mixture and let it slowly heat-up. Do not let boil.

   Serve over mashed potatoes and grain dishes.

Sun Dried Tomato Pesto

8+ Servings

1 C sun dried tomatoes,
   soaked in water
2 pitted dates
½ C basil leaves, tightly packed
1 T nutritional yeast

2 cloves garlic, pressed
2 T chopped red onion,
½ C macadamia or pine nuts, soaked
1 Roma tomato
1 T white miso

   Place all ingredients in a food processor and blend to desired consistency.
   A superior accompaniment to many dishes and a great sauce for polenta.

Sweet Ginger Dipping Sauce
4–6 servings

¼ C toasted sesame oil
¼ C toasted peanuts or mac nuts,
   finely chopped
2 T rice vinegar
2 T fresh lime or lemon juice

1 T finely grated fresh ginger
1 T agave nectar
2 tsp tamari
1 tsp curry powder
2 cloves garlic, finely grated or pressed

In a small bowl, put all the ingredients and stir together.
Serve with Jia's Summer Rolls (p. 121).

Tahini Sauce
10 servings

1½ C warm water
2 cloves garlic, minced
1 C roasted tahini
Juice of one large lemon
½ tsp ground coriander

½ tsp ground cumin
1 tsp crystal salt
pinch black pepper
3 dashes hot sauce

Combine all ingredients in a blender, or whisk until smooth.

Teriyaki Marinade
2 large servings

2 T tamari
2 T sesame oil
1 T maple syrup or agave nectar

2 T rice vinegar
2 T ginger, grated
1 T garlic, finely grated

Mix all ingredients together.

Vegan Raita
4+ servings

1 block firm or med. tofu (18 oz)
¼ C soy or rice mylk
2 cloves garlic, pressed (Optional)
1 T finely grated ginger
2 tsp cumin powder
1 tsp coriander powder

1½ lemons, juiced
¼ C safflower oil
1 T tamari
1 T maple syrup
1 T fresh mint, finely chopped
1 large zucchini, grated

In a food processor, blend all ingredients except mint and zucchini to a creamy consistency. Mix with remaining ingredients. Yum

Walnut Sage Sauce
8 servings

Sautéed Leek
1 tsp grape seed oil
1 small leek, diced small
1 clove garlic, finely grated or pressed

Walnut Mixture
2 C water
½ C raw walnuts, soaked 12 hours
¼ C white spelt flour or barley flour
1 T arrowroot powder
1 T fresh lemon juice
3 T finely chopped fresh sage leaves

Sautéed Leek: In a medium sauce pan, slowly heat the oil. Add the leek and garlic and sauté until tender, about 5 min.

Walnut Mixture: In a blender, put all the ingredients for the Walnut Mixture and blend until smooth.
Pour the blended Walnut Mixture in with the Sautéed Leek and simmer until thick, about 2 minutes
Serve over Zucchini Love Boats
(p. 145)

 # *Soups*

Best Borscht
6 servings

8 C water
2 C beets, diced
½ medium cabbage, chopped
3 large carrots, chopped
1½ onions, chopped
2 medium potatoes, diced

1 or 2 bay leaves
1 tsp garlic powder
1 T dill weed
2 tsp crystal salt
1 tsp black pepper

Place all ingredients in a large, covered soup pot and bring to boil.
Reduce heat and simmer for 45–60 minutes. Oh, so good!
Serve with a dollop of Tofu Sour Cream (p. 83) and chopped chives.

Creamy Carrot Yam Soup
4 servings

1 medium garnet yam
4 large carrots
1 T sesame oil
1 T coconut oil
1 large onion or leek, chopped
1 T fresh ginger, minced
½ tsp pepper
½ tsp nutmeg
1 tsp coriander
4 C water
1 T Bernard Jensens veggie stock
   powder
1 T white miso
½ C cashews, soaked

Peel and chop yams and carrots.

Using a 2 quart soup pot, sauté onion and ginger in oil, on medium heat for 4 minutes.

Add spices and cook for 2 more minutes.

Add the yams, carrots, water and veggies to the pot and bring to a light boil. Cook until veggies are soft, then turn off heat.

Blend miso, cashews and half the soup in a blender, return to pot, mix and serve.

When reheating be sure to use medium-low heat to preserve miso's enzymes.

Cream of Broccoli Soup
6 servings

4 C water
4 medium Yukon gold or yellow finn
  potatoes, cut in ½" cubes
1 medium leek,
  white and green parts, sliced
2 stalks broccoli, trimmed
  and coarsely chopped

Cashew Cream
1 C raw cashews or blanched almonds
2 C water
1 tsp crystal salt
2 T fresh lemon juice
  fresh ground black pepper, to taste

In a large pot, put the 4 cups water, cover and bring to a boil. Add the potatoes, cover and simmer 3 minutes. Add the leek and simmer 3 more minutes. Add the broccoli and simmer until the vegetables are tender, about 3 more minutes.

Cashew Cream
In a blender, put the cashews and blend into a crumbly meal. Through the hole in the blender lid, slowly add the water, salt and lemon juice. Blend until smooth and creamy.

Stop the blender. Add the cooked soup and blend until creamy smooth. The soup will have to be blended in 2 or 3 batches.

Pour the blended soup mixture into a large pot and heat, do not boil. Adjust seasonings. Add the black pepper to taste.

> *I do not know what your destiny will be, but this I do know, the only ones among you who will be truly happy are those who have sought and found a way to serve.*
>
> Albert Schweitzer

Creamy Potato Vegetable Soup
8 servings

2 T olive oil
2 onions, chopped
6 cloves garlic, minced
4 stalks celery, chopped
6 C water, boiling
2 bay leaves
2 T Bronner's veggie powder
3 lbs potatoes, peeled and cubed
1 large leek, washed and sliced
2 carrots, chopped
1 head cauliflower, chopped
2 C soy milk (or other)
2 T nutritional yeast
½ tsp sage powder
1 T fresh tarragon, chopped
1 tsp red pepper flakes
1 tsp black pepper
¼ C miso
Parsley leaves, chopped

In a large soup pot, heat oil and sauté garlic, celery and onions until translucent. Add boiling water, then all ingredients except carrots and cauliflower, and simmer.

To wash leeks, slice and rinse, being sure to wash in between all the layers.

When potatoes start to soften (10 minutes), add leek and carrots & cook until carrots begin to soften.

Add cauliflower & cook 3 more minutes.

Transfer ⅓ of soup and all the mylk to a food processor or blender.

Add spices and miso, blend until smooth, then mix back into the soup pot. Garnish with fresh parsley.

This Earth is precious to Him, and to harm the Earth is to heap contempt on its creator. The whites too shall pass, perhaps sooner than all other tribes. Contaminate your bed, and you will one night suffocate in your own waste.

Chief Seattle's Address, 1854

Gardens' Coconut Mana Soup
8 yummy servings

2 cans coconut milk
1 medium Kabocha squash,
  either baked or steamed.
2" ginger, finely chopped and
  divided into 2 portions
1 whole garlic bulb baked ½ hour
2 T sesame oil
1 small leek, chopped
1 tsp yellow curry paste
¾ C white miso
2 C water

Blend coconut milk with squash, half of the ginger, and baked garlic that has been squeezed from the peel. Slowly heat in a 1 gallon pot on medium heat.

In a medium sauté pan, heat oil and sauté remaining ginger, leek, and yellow curry paste.

Lightly blend the sauté with water and miso and add into soup. If soup is too thick, add more water, soy or coconut milk.

This delicious soup is a nourishing favorite with retreat groups and residents at the Sanctuary of Mana Ke'a Gardens in South Kona.

> *Our experience of pain for the world springs from our inter-connectedness with all beings, from which also arises our powers to act on their behalf. When we deny or repress our pain for the world, or treat it as a private pathology, our power to take part in the healing of our world is diminished.*
>
> www.Joannamacy.net

Golden Split Pea Soup
6 servings

Tamari Toasted Sunnies
1 C sunflower seeds, soaked 1 hour
2 T tamari
1 pinch cayenne pepper

Split Pea Soup
6 C water
1 C yellow split peas, rinsed well
5 new potatoes, diced large

3 ribs celery with leaves, sliced
2 medium carrots, sliced in ¼" rounds
1 yellow onion, diced large
2 cloves garlic, finely grated or pressed
½ C coarsely chopped fresh parsley
   leaves
3 T tamari
2 T fresh lemon juice

Tamari Toasted Sunnies: In a small frying pan, over medium heat, put the soaked sunflower seeds and toast, stirring often until a golden color, for 10 to 15 minutes. While the seeds are still in the pan and the pan is still hot, add the tamari and cayenne. Stir until the tamari has completely evaporated. Put into a small bowl and set aside.

Split Pea Soup: In a large pot, add the 6 cups water and rinsed split peas. Bring to a boil, turn down the heat and simmer until peas are almost tender, about 35 minutes. Add the potatoes, celery, carrots, onion and garlic. Cook until tender, about 15 minutes. Remove from the heat, add the parsley, tamari and lemon juice. Stir to mix. Sprinkle the Tamari Toasted Sunnies over the top of each serving.

> *But those who know the secret of nature, those who see everywhere in nature the Oneness that is beyond nature, they alone enjoy Eternal Bliss.*
>
> The Upanishads, translated by Juan Mascaro

Lemon Lentil Soup

6 servings

7 C water
1 C green lentils, washed
4 new potatoes, peeled and cut in ¼-inch cubes
2 ribs celery and leaves, sliced small
2 medium carrots, diced small
1 medium yellow onion, diced small
2 cloves garlic, grated small or pressed

1 small bunch Swiss chard or kale, de-stemmed and chopped
½ C finely chopped fresh parsley leaves
3 T tamari
2 T fresh lemon juice
1 ½ tsp cumin powder
pinch of cayenne

In a large pot, put the 7 cups water and washed lentils. Cover and simmer until almost tender, about 35 minutes. Add the potatoes, celery, carrots, onion and garlic and simmer until tender, about 8 minutes. Remove from the heat, add the remaining ingredients and stir to mix.

Store in a covered glass container in the refrigerator for up to 4 days.

That no one on Earth can be truly happy as long as he keeps causing harm to the Earth.

Anastasia's words from "The Space of Love" by Vladimir Megre, translated by John Woodsworth. Ringing Cedars Press 2005

Marvelous Millet Soup
6 servings

Sautéed Mushrooms
1 T grape seed oil
1 yellow onion, diced small
½ pound Shiitake mushrooms, sliced
3 cloves garlic, grated fine or pressed

Soup
4 C water
½ C millet
3 carrots, diced small
3 ribs celery and leaves, diced small
½ small cauliflower, cut in small florets
1 T finely chopped fresh rosemary
1 teaspoon finely chopped fresh thyme
3 C soy or almond mylk
¼ cup nutritional yeast flakes
2 T fresh lemon juice
3 T tamari

Sautéed Mushrooms: In a large frying pan, slowly heat the oil. Add the onion and sauté for 3 minutes. Add the mushrooms and garlic and sauté until tender, about 4 more minutes.

Soup: In a large pot, put the 4 cups water, cover and bring to a boil. Add the millet, cover and simmer until almost tender, about 20 minutes. Add the carrot and celery and simmer 3 more minutes. Add the cauliflower, cover and simmer until the vegetables are tender, about 4 more minutes. Add the remaining ingredients and the Sautéed Mushrooms. Stir to mix, then gently heat but do not boil.

The vibratory harmony and balanced nutrition of a sattvik diet— restraining any temptation toward greed or overeating—promotes not only good health, vitality, and longevity; but also works on the mind to nurture a calm, contented, cheerful disposition inclined toward goodness and spiritual aspirations.

Paramahansa Yogananda,
The Bhagavad Gita, Royal Science of God Realization

Potato Beet Soup
8 servings

4 garlic cloves, chopped
1 ½ onions, chopped

1 T basil, dried
2 tsp thyme, dried
2 large carrots, sliced
8 medium beets (2 lbs), peeled
    and sliced into ½" pieces

1 lb red potatoes, cubed
8 C water
2 vegetable stock cubes
2 T tamari
½ tsp black pepper, fresh ground

2 T fresh parsley, finely chopped

In a medium soup pot, heat oil and sauté garlic and onion for 3 to 4 minutes on medium high heat.

Add basil, thyme, carrots and beets and sauté for another 5 minutes.

Add potatoes, water and veggie stock cubes, and simmer until the potatoes are cooked (about 20 minutes).

Remove half the ingredients and blend in a blender with pepper and tamari.

Return to pot and garnish with fresh parsley. Serve with Almond Pesto (p. 91).

The term "deep ecology" was coined by the Norwegian professor of Philosophy and eco-activist Arne Naess, and has been taken up by academics and environmentalists in Europe, the US and Australia. The essence of deep ecology is to ask deeper questions.... We ask which society, which education, which form of religion is beneficial for all life on the planet as a whole.

www.Joannamacy.net

Potato Corn Chowder

4 servings

Soup
4 C water
4 medium Yukon Gold or Yellow Finn potatoes, cut in ½" cubes
2 stalks celery, sliced
1 medium leek, white and green parts, sliced and cleaned well
2 C corn, fresh or frozen
Rind of ½ lemon, left intact
Fresh ground black pepper, to taste

Cashew Corn Cream
1 C raw cashews or blanched almonds
2 C water
1 C corn kernels, fresh or frozen
1 tsp crystal salt
2 T fresh lemon juice

Soup: In a large pot, put the 4 cups water, cover and bring to a boil. Add the potatoes, cover and simmer 3 minutes. Add the celery and simmer 3 more minutes. Add the leek and simmer until the vegetables are tender, about 4 more minutes. Add the 2 cups corn and lemon rind.

Cashew Corn Cream: In a blender, put all ingredients for the Cashew Corn Cream and blend until smooth. If needed, add more water so mixture flows freely through the blender blade.

Add the Cashew Corn Cream to the Soup and stir. Gently heat but do not boil.

Raw Avocado Soup

2 servings

1 C almond mylk
1 medium avocado
1 C water
1 T white miso
1 C cucumber, grated
1 C zucchini, grated
1 T parsley, chopped
1 T cilantro *or* basil,
   chopped
Dulse, for topping

Blend first 4 ingredients and half of the next 4 ingredients.

Add remaining portions, garnishing top with fresh herbs.

Serve either at room temperature or chilled.

The variations on this raw soup are endless.
Here are some of the possibilities:
Fresh carrot juice or any fresh juice for the liquid.
Add fresh corn to soup or base. Add other vegetables such as sunflower sprouts, red pepper, tomato, etc.
For heat, add ⅛ tsp crushed red pepper.

Raw Tomato Soup

2 servings

4 medium tomatoes, chopped
2 T green onion stalks, chopped
1 tsp basil, minced
1 tsp thyme, minced
Juice of ½ lemon
½ small avocado
½ cucumber chopped

Optional:
1 clove garlic
¼ C cashews (soaked 1 hour)
¼ C raw fresh corn
2 C carrot, celery, beet juice
¼ C sprouts
¼ C grated zucchini

Blend all ingredients well. Pour over sprouts or zucchini.
Garnish Options: 1 tsp chopped fresh parsley, 1 tsp kelp flakes, 1 T dulse flakes

Raw Super Soup by Isabel

4 servings
Best made in a Vita Mix blender!

2 large cucumbers
1 large handful tender kale
1 medium avocado
1 red bell pepper
1 T Vitamineral Greens powder
1 tsp maca powder

1 tsp flax seeds
1 T hemp protein powder
1 T hemp seeds
Water or nut/seed mylk to blend

Blend well into soup like consistency. When serving, add chunks of avocado, apple pieces, assorted sprouts (sunflower, mung, lentil).

Raw Avocado Cucumber Soup

4 servings (about one and one half cups per serving)

2 C water
1 medium avocado, quartered
4 tomatillos, quartered
1 medium cucumber, cut in large
   chunks
2 green onions, white and green parts,
   cut large

½ C fresh cilantro leaves
3 T fresh lime or lemon juice
½ tsp chili sauce
½ tsp crystal salt
½ medium cucumber, diced small

In a blender, put all the ingredients, except the diced cucumber, and blend until creamy smooth.

Pour the soup into chilled individual bowls. Add an equal amount of the diced cucumber to each bowl of soup and a few leaves of cilantro for a garnish. Best served soon after making.

Simply Delicious Miso Soup
Makes 4 cups

Stock
4 C water
½ C dried Shitaki mushrooms
2 8-inch by 2-inch strips of Kombu
    seaweed
1 T chopped ginger
I C Kabocha squash, in small chunks
Opt: 1 6-inch piece lemongrass

Vegetables
½ C chopped green onion
1 C Westbrae or similar pre-cooked
    and flavored Tofu

Miso Mixture
In a small bowl, put all ingredients for
the Miso Mixture and whisk together.

Miso Mixture
1 C water
¼ C white miso or other miso
2 T fresh lemon juice

In a medium soup pot, add 4 C water,
mushrooms, kabocha chunks, kombu
and ginger (also optional lemon grass),
cover and bring to a boil. Lower heat
and simmer for 15 minutes. Add green
onions and tofu, and simmer for a
few more minutes. Remove kombu,
mushrooms and optional lemongrass,
then add Miso Mixture.

Opt: Add a tsp of Thai Kitchen Spicy Red Chile Sauce or hot sesame oil.
Add any other vegetables at appropriate times during cooking process.

---

*Vegetarians have the best diet. They have the lowest rates of coronary
disease of any group in the country. Some people scoff at vegetarians, but
they have a fraction of our heart attack rate and they have only 40% of
our cancer rate. They outlive us. On the average they outlive other men by
about six years now.*

W. Castelli, quoted in *Diet for a New America,* John Robbins

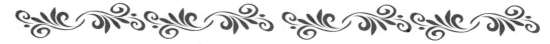

Thai Coconut Cauliflower Soup
4 servings

¾ C coconut milk
2 5" stalks lemon grass, cleaned
1" fresh ginger, finely chopped
1 tsp Kefir lime leaves, finely chopped
2 T tamari or miso
2 tsp sweetener
1 T vegetable stock powder
4 C water
½ tsp crushed red pepper flakes
1 medium cauliflower, cut into florets
¼ w. cabbage, shredded
2 fresh tomatoes, cubed
2 T fresh lemon juice
4 T fresh cilantro, chopped

Bring all ingredients, except last 3 to a boil over medium heat in a 2-quart pot.

Reduce heat and simmer for 10 minutes

Add tomatoes cauliflower and cabbage for the last few minutes of simmering until cauliflower is tender.. Remove lemon grass stalks

Stir in lemon juice and garnish with cilantro.

Some tasty variations include adding carrots, green beans, or vegetables of choice, paying attention to varying cooking times.

The planet is in bad political shape and is administered appallingly. An outer space inspection team would undoubtedly give us an F (Failure) or a triple D (Dumb, Deficient and Dangerous) in planetary management. Our world is afflicted by a good dozen conflicts almost permanently. Its skies, land and ocean are infested with atomic weapons which cost $850 billion dollars a year, while so many poor people are dying of hunger on the planet....

Robert Muller, Former UN assistant Secretary General
Assistant Chancellor, University of Peace, *Planethood: The Key to Your Future,* Benjamin B. Ferenz, Ken Keyes, Jr.

Todd's Thyme Soup
6 servings

2 T olive oil
2 onions, diced
8 cloves garlic, peeled and
  chopped
2 T fresh thyme, chopped
½ tsp crushed red pepper
½ C celery, chopped

8 C boiling water
2 vegetable stock cubes
8 medium yellow potatoes,
  washed and chopped
½ lb carrots, peeled and chopped
½ lb chard or spinach, chopped
½ C brown rice miso

In a large pot, sauté onions and garlic in oil until onions are soft. Add thyme, celery, and pepper and sauté for a few more minutes.

Dissolve vegetable stock cubes in boiling water and add to the soup pot a cup or two at a time, adding potatoes and carrots as well. Cook for about 15 minutes.

Add chopped greens and cook for another few minutes.

Turn soup off. Remove ⅓ cup of the stock and mix with miso, and as much potatoes as possible to blend well. Return to the pot and serve.

A great winter soup and an excellent way to use up leftover vegetables.

Eradicating self-destructive dietary and lifestyle habits is a task equivalent to breaking free from drug addiction. The majority of people who try to go halfway will remain in the trap. An extreme, short-term commitment to healthful living can give you the invaluable experience of what it feels like to be free from the trap.

Douglas L. Lislie, Ph.D., Alan Goldhamer, D.C., *The Pleasure Trap*

 # Vegetables

Ayurvedic Indian Vegetables

6–8 servings

4 T oil (coconut, sesame, grape seed)
1 tsp mixed fenugreek, mustard
  and onion seeds
2 medium onions, sliced
4 medium potatoes, cubed
4 carrots, chopped

¼ C tomato paste
1 tsp chili powder

1 T fresh ginger, chopped
1 tsp coriander, ground
1 T tamari
½ C coconut milk
2 T shredded coconut
1 C frozen peas, thawed
½ cauliflower, cut into florets
2 T cilantro, chopped
1 oz lemon juice

In a large frying pan, heat oil to medium-high, add seeds, then onions. Lower heat, adding potatoes, then carrots. Sauté for a few minutes. Add tomato paste, chili powder, ginger, coriander, tamari, and coconut milk. Continue cooking on a medium-low simmer until almost done. Add coconut, peas, and cauliflower and cook until tender. Add lemon juice and cilantro at the end.

> *It is good to prepare vegetables with real appreciation for what you are doing, thus enabling the radiations of light to enter the food. A potato is no longer just a potato in your hands, but a thing of real beauty. You can feel it is something living, vibrating. Just stop and think what a difference this makes to the vegetables. Sometimes you feel your heart will burst with joy and appreciation.*
>
> Eileen's guidance, *The Findhorn Family Cookbook,*
> by Kay Lynne Sherman, Findhorn Press

Coconut, Cinnamon Squash or Yam

4–6 servings

1 medium Kabocha squash or
    4 yams, pre-cooked
1 T coconut oil
2 T Artemesa Coconut Butter
2 tsp cinnamon
1 tsp pumpkin pie spice
1 T agave or maple syrup
½ tsp crystal salt

Bake squash or yam whole, then remove skin and seeds if squash.
In a small pan with medium heat, warm rest of ingredients.
Mix with chunks of squash or glaze halved lengthwise yams and re-bake in oven at 350° for 15 minutes.
Opt: Place all ingredients in food processor and mix to a mashed potato consistency.

Excellent served as a fine compliment to Forbidden Rice (p. 130) or Wild Rice Medley (p.144), or add either rice vegetable mixture to large baking dish, cover with squash or yam mashed mixture and bake for 15 minutes at 375°.

Caraway Cabbage

4 servings

½ tsp caraway seeds
2 T safflower or grape seed oil
1 tsp garam masala
½ tsp coriander powder
4 medium tomatoes, chopped
½ tsp turmeric powder
½ tsp black pepper flakes
1 small cabbage finely shredded/
    steamed
1 cup frozen peas, defrosted
½ C plain soy milk
1 tsp crystal salt
2 T fresh dill, finely chopped

In a large sauté pan on medium high heat cook caraway seeds in oil for a minute.

Add next 2 spices and tomatoes and cook for 2 more minutes.

Add rest of ingredients (except dill), turn heat to medium and cook until cabbage is tender. About 5 minutes. Garnish with dill.

Creamy Cashew Tomato Curry
4–6 servings

½ C cashews, soaked 2 hours
1½ C water
2 T coconut oil
1 onion, chopped
1 T finely grated ginger
4 cloves garlic, finely chopped
1 tsp cumin seeds

1 tsp coriander seeds, fresh ground
1 tsp curry powder
1 potato in small cooked chunks
4 tomatoes, chopped
2 C assorted vegetables, steamed
½ C chopped cilantro
2 tsp crystal salt

Blend cashews with water and set aside. Sauté cumin seeds with onion, ginger and garlic for a few minutes. Add rest of spices and cook a while longer. Add rest of ingredients including cashew mix, bring to a simmer and turn off heat.

Naturopathic Philosophy

Respect the healing power of Nature.

Remove obstacles to the cure.

Identify and treat the cause of illness.

First do no harm. (Use the least invasive treatment.)

Treat the whole person.

Emphasize wellness.

Remember that prevention is the best cure.

Stress the role of the physician as the teacher.

Dr. Laurie Steelsmith, "Natural Choices for Women's Health"

Coconut Rice
6 servings

2 T (raw) coconut oil
1 T ginger, minced or grated
1 onion, chopped
1 T Super Spice (p. 83)

¾ C w. Basmati rice, washed & rinsed
¾ C quinoa, washed & rinsed
1 can coconut milk (15 oz)
2 C water
2 T agave nectar
1 red bell pepper, chopped
¼ C mint leaves, finely chopped
4 med tomatoes, chopped
1 C green peas
¼ C cashews, chopped
¼ C raisins

¼ C flaked coconut, roasted

In a 1.5 quart sauce pan on medium high heat add oil, onion and ginger. Cook for a few minutes, add spice and cook for 1 more minute.

Add coconut milk, water and agave nectar and bring to rolling boil. Add rice mixture and bring back to boil.

Immediately turn to low, cover, and simmer for 15 minutes.

Add rest of ingredients to top of pot. close lid and cook 5 more minutes then shut off heat, stir well and let stand 5 more minutes.

Lightly roast coconut flakes for a few minutes, stirring often in a dry sauté pan on medium heat.
Garnish with coconut flakes

A revolution is underway because people are realizing that our needs can be met without destroying our world. We have the technical knowledge, the communication tools, and material resources to grow enough food, ensure clean air and water, and meet rational energy needs.

www.Joannamacy.net

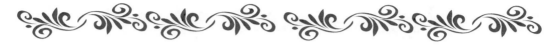

Cornbread
Makes a 9-inch square

Peppers
1 medium red bell pepper, left whole
1 jalapeño pepper, left whole

Dry Mixture
1 C cornmeal
1 C white spelt or barley flour
1 tsp baking powder
1 tsp baking soda
½ tsp crystal salt

Wet Mixture
1 C rice beverage or soy milk
¼ C olive oil
2 T fresh lemon juice
1 ear corn, cut off cob, or 1 cup frozen corn kernels

Preheat oven to 400º F. Lightly oil a 9 x 9-inch glass baking dish and dust with cornmeal.

Peppers: On a baking sheet lined with kitchen parchment paper, put the red bell pepper and jalapeño. Bake at 400º F for 15 minutes. Remove the jalapeño pepper from the oven and set aside to cool. Turn the bell pepper over and continue to bake until a little black on top, about 15 more minutes, then remove from oven and set aside until cool enough to handle. When cool enough to handle, peel the peppers. Small dice the bell pepper and mince the jalapeño, using as many seeds and white tissue parts as you like for hotness.

Dry Mixture: In a large mixing bowl, put all the Dry Mixture and stir together

Wet Mixture: In a small bowl, put all the Wet Mixture and stir together.

Pour the Wet Mixture over the Dry Mixture and stir to mix. Add the prepared peppers and stir again. Spoon the batter into the prepared baking dish.
Bake at 350º F until done, about 40 minutes. The bread is done when a wooden toothpick inserted near the center comes out clean.
Let the bread cool for 10 minutes before cutting into squares and serving.

Curried Potato "Fries"
2 servings

1 T grape seed oil
1 tsp curry powder
½ tsp cumin seeds
½ tsp crystal salt

2 cloves garlic, grated small or pressed
6 to 8 new potatoes or 2 large baking
  potatoes, cut in large wedges

Preheat the oven to 400º F. Lightly oil a baking sheet or cover with kitchen parchment paper.

In a large mixing bowl, put all the ingredients, except the potatoes, and stir together. Add the potatoes and stir until the potatoes are well coated with the seasonings.

Spread the seasoned potatoes on the prepared baking sheet. The potatoes can touch each other, but do not let them overlap.

Put on the middle rack of the oven. Bake at 400º F for 15 minutes. Turn the potatoes over and bake until they are tender when poked with a fork, 10 to 15 more minutes.

Turn the oven to broil. Put the potatoes under the broiler, leaving the oven door open a crack. Let the potatoes broil until they are puffy and brown on top, 1 to 2 minutes. Keep a watchful eye on the potatoes so they do not burn.

> *Whatever befalls the Earth befalls the sons of the Earth. Man did not weave the web of life; he is merely a strand of it. Whatever he does to the web, he does to himself.*
>
> Chief Seattle's Address, 1854

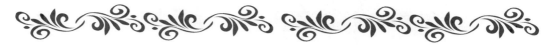

Green Beans with Ginger & Macadamia Nuts

8 servings

½ lb green beans
¼ lb raw mac nuts
1" ginger, peeled
1 T sesame oil
1 T coconut oil
1 large onion, sliced
2 T tamari

Cut off stem ends and slice green beans into thirds and steam until just tender. Rough chop mac nuts in food processor. Cut ginger into pieces and fine chop. Sauté onion and ginger in oil over medium-high heat, adding tamari at the end. Add beans and nuts and sauté together for a couple more minutes.

Another delicious Option is to add sliced mushrooms cooked with the onions.
A simple and satisfying dish!

Herb Roasted Potatoes

12 servings

6 lbs potatoes – combination of red, purple and orange sweet potatoes or yams.
¼ C fresh thyme, chopped
2 T fresh oregano, chopped
1 T Simply Organic All Purpose Seasoning
12 cloves fresh garlic, finely minced
4 T olive oil
4 T tamari

Bake potatoes at 375° for 45 minutes or until just soft. Cut into bite sized chunks removing any rough or hard skin.

Combine remaining ingredients and toss with potatoes. Place in a large baking dish and rebake at 375° for 20 minutes or until crispy around the edges. Toss once or twice during cooking process to insure even cooking.

Serve with tofu sour cream (p. 83)
Any leftovers can be used to make the best sweet potato salad ever.

Italian Vegetables
8 servings
Italian Vegetable Stir-Fry

½ lb green beans
1½ heads broccoli
2 zucchinis
2 T olive oil
1 onion, chopped
6 cloves garlic, peeled and chopped
¼ C sun-dried tomatoes, chopped
4 medium tomatoes, chopped
1 T fresh thyme leaves, minced
1 T fresh oregano, minced
1 T fresh marjoram, minced
2 T tamari

Cut green beans, broccoli, and zucchini into bite-sized pieces, then lightly steam, starting with the longer cooking beans. Set aside.

Sauté onion and garlic in olive oil.

When onions become translucent, add the remaining ingredients and lightly cook for a minute or two.

Add steamed veggies and continue cooking for another couple of minutes, stirring occasionally.

Serve with Peaceful Pesto Sauce (p. 95)

Ancient Prayer
Sarvepi sukhinah bhavam, sarve santu niramayah
May all beings be happy, may all beings be free from fear

And all of this because of a limited sense of welfare, an inability to grasp the unity of all things, a stubborn refusal to accept the Earth not as a material object to be manipulated at will, but a shining spiritual entity.

Karan Singh, *At Home in the Universe*

Jia's Summer Rolls
4 + servings

1 package rice papers
2 med. carrots, grated large
1 English cucumber, cut in
  matchsticks
1 med. head leaf lettuce,
  finely shredded
1 C finely chopped fresh mint
1 C finely chopped cilantro

Fill a large bowl with warm water and immerse a rice paper until soft, about 1 minute. Lay the rice paper on a dry towel and put a little of each salad ingredient horizontally on the rice paper. Drizzle with the Sweet Ginger Dipping Sauce. Roll-up the salad by first folding the right and left sides up and over the salad. Then starting with the side closest to you, tightly roll-up the rice paper over the salad. Repeat with remaining ingredients.

Serve with Sweet Ginger Dipping Sauce (p. 97)

Moroccan Carrots
4 servings

1 lb carrots
2 cloves garlic, pressed
½ tsp cinnamon powder
½ tsp cumin powder
Pinch cayenne pepper
2 tsp agave nectar
½ tsp crystal salt
2 T olive oil
2 T lemon juice
1 T fresh parsley, chopped

Peel and chop carrots, then steam until tender.

Mix the rest of the ingredients into a dressing and marinate carrots for 1 hour.

Serve at room temperature or chilled.

Ma's Khicharie

1 T coconut oil
1 tsp cumin and fennel seeds
Dash of fenugreek
1 C white Basmati rice, rinsed
½ C baby red lentils, cleaned
3½ C boiling water
1 tsp turmeric powder
2 C mixed vegetables, carrots etc.
2 medium red potatoes, chopped
1 tsp crystal salt

In a 2 quart pot sauté spices in coconut oil for 3 minutes
Add water and bring to a boil, then add lentils, rice, and turmeric and bring to a boil again
Chop vegetables, and add all ingredients.
Return to a boil, cover, turn heat to low, and cook for 20 to 25 minutes.
Opt: ½ C mixed raisins and chopped cashews may be added after 15 minutes for extra flavor.

You will find Her whom you sought, nearer than the nearest, the very breath of life, the very core of every heart.

Anandamayee Ma

Mega Wrap

Tortillas– Ezekial, sprouted or rice
leftover cooked quinoa or rice,
Tofu, tempeh, or other protein
Salad greens & sprouts

Vegenaise or Tofu Mayo (p. 83)
Simply Excellent Dressing (p. 77)
  or dressing of choice
Nutritional yeast
Avocado, in chunks or slices

Opt: cooked squash, toasted nuts
and seeds, dulse

Romaine lettuce leaves or nori
sheets may be used in place of
tortillas for a similar dish.

Lightly warm or toast tortilla.
Warm grain / veggie dish using a steamer
or sauté with some oil and fresh garlic.

Use precooked tofu or make basic tofu,
tempeh, tempeh bacon or other protein.

Spread Vegenaise on the tortilla and layer
the middle with ingredients of choice.

Add salad dressing or dress with splashes
of oil, lemon, soy, tamari, etc.

To wrap, place thumbs under tortilla and
bring the side closest to you over the top,
pulling and sliding and gently squeezing
all ingredients to one end with your
fingers. Fold one side over and tightly roll.
Practice makes perfect.

One of our most favorite and reliable dishes.
A quick, simple, balanced "fast food" meal for home or on the go.

*Studies in Campbell's laboratory and elsewhere have demonstrated
that without animal proteins in the diet the initiation process of cancer
development is often stalled. It appears that regardless of the level of exposure of the initiating carcinogen, many cancers may be unable to develop
and progress without the presence of animal protein in the diet!*

Douglas L. Lislie, Ph.D., Alan Goldhamer D.C., *The Pleasure Trap*

Spiced Kale
2 servings

½ lb young kale leaves, washed,
    stems removed and shredded.
2 T coconut oil
1 T ginger, minced
½ tsp fennel seed
½ tsp cumin seed

1 T tamari
¼ C cashews, chopped
¼ C sun-dried tomatoes, chopped
½ tsp garam masala
½ tsp crushed red pepper

In a large sauté pan on medium high heat, add oil, ginger, fennel and cumin, then cook for 3 minutes.

Add kale and tamari and cook covered for a few minutes stirring occasionally.

Turn heat to medium, add cashews and sun dried tomatoes and continue cooking covered, stirring occasionally for a few more minutes.

Add rest of spices. Mix well, turn off heat and let stand for a few more minutes

Spicy Corn with Red Peppers
4–6 servings

2 T safflower or grape seed oil
1 onion, chopped
2 cloves garlic, chopped

1 pinch cayenne or jalapeno pepper
2 C fresh or frozen kernel corn
1 medium red bell pepper, seeded
    and chopped
1 tomato, chopped
¼ C soy or nut mylk

2 T white miso
¼ C toasted pine or mac nuts

Sauté onion and garlic on medium-heat for 1 minute.

Add corn and peppers and sauté for a couple minutes more.

Add tomato and soy milk, reduce heat and simmer for a couple more minutes.

Blend miso in ½ cup of the liquid and return to pot.

Mix well and serve with a sprinkling of toasted nuts.

Stir-Fry Vegetable Curry

1 T sesame oil
1 T grape seed or coconut oil
1 medium onion, finely chopped
2" ginger, minced
2 medium garnet yams, peeled,
  halved lengthwise, then thin sliced
½ C water
½ bunch dinosaur kale, shredded
¼ red cabbage, finely chopped
2 med. carrots, in matchsticks
2 T tamari
1 T curry powder
1 tsp allspice powder
1 medium head broccoli, chopped
½ C cashews

On medium heat, sauté onion, ginger and yams in oil for a couple of minutes.

Add water, kale, cabbage, carrots, tamari, curry and allspice, continue cooking, covered.

Add broccoli, cashews and more water if needed and cook until just tender, stirring often.

A lid will keep heat in and allow for more even cooking.

Other vegetables and herbs of choice may be added

This dish is excellent served with grain such as quinoa or jasmine rice.

The very food product systems that are providing us with the foods that medical science is finding are harming our health—the very same factory farms and feedlots that are so painfully cruel to animals—are also, as it turns out, undermining the life-support systems of our imperiled planet.

John Robbins, *The Food Revolution*

Thai Vegetables with Noodles
4 servings

1 can coconut milk
½ tsp yellow curry paste
2 tsp Sucanat or Rapadura
1 C green beans, cut into 1" pieces
1 red bell pepper, cut into 2" strips
8 oz rice noodles, barely cooked
4 oz mung bean sprouts
1 T brown rice miso
¼ C mac nuts or almonds,
    roasted & chopped
2 T fresh cilantro, chopped

In a medium size pan, gently heat coconut milk, curry paste and sweetener over medium heat.

Add beans and simmer until they are almost tender (10 minutes).

Add all ingredients, except last 3 and simmer for 2 more minutes. Add miso and garnish with roasted nuts and cilantro.

If desired, sauté 1 chopped onion and 2 cloves garlic before adding coco mylk.

Zucchini & Mushrooms in White Sauce
4-6 servings

2 T safflower oil
1 large onion, chopped

1 tsp coriander powder
1 tsp cumin powder
2 T tamari
½ tsp chili powder
8 mushrooms, sliced
2 medium zucchinis
¼ C soy mylk
2 T nutritional yeast
2 T cilantro, chopped

Sauté onions on medium-high in a frying pan. When onions are soft, lower heat to medium and add spices, cooking until well blended.

Add tamari and mushrooms and cook until almost tender (5 min).

Quarter zucchini lengthwise and slice into 1" pieces.

Add zucchini, soy mylk and yeast and lightly cook until zucchini's are done.

Serve with chopped cilantro for a delightful treat.

Main Courses

Asian Tofu Vegetable Delight
4-6 servings

1 T unrefined sesame oil
2 T coconut or safflower oil
2" ginger, finely chopped
1 onion, chopped
1 lb tofu, in small cubes

1 C fresh shiitake mushrooms,
  chopped
1 red bell pepper, chopped
1 T coriander powder
2 T tamari
⅛ C water

¼ lb snow peas, tips removed
8 oz mung bean sprouts
1 T nutritional yeast
2 tsp Thai Kitchen spicy red chili sauce
2 tsp chopped cilantro

Preheat oven to 375°

Mix all ingredients except for last four in a medium glass baking dish.

Bake covered for 20 minutes then uncover and stir well.

Bake 10 more minutes, add remaining ingredients except cilantro, mix well and bake 5 more minutes.

Remove from oven, garnish with cilantro, stir and serve.

Excellent with Gombu sauce (p. 92)

Fortunately, many people do see the underlying cause of the health care crisis. They realize that the main causes of disease in this country are diet and lifestyle. In fact, nearly seventy percent of us die from diet-and-lifestyle-related diseases.

Dr. Terry Shintani, M.D., J.D., M.P.H., "The Hawaii Diet"

5th Mindfulness Training

Aware of the suffering caused by unmindful consumption, I am committed to cultivate good health, both physical and mental for myself, my family, and my society by practicing mindful eating, drinking, and consuming. I am committed to ingest only items that preserve peace, well being and joy in my consciousness....

Thich Nhat Hahn, *Going Home: Jesus and Buddha as Brothers*

Buddha Balls
24 balls

2 C cooked short grain rice, warm
1 pound firm tofu, mashed
4 T brown rice miso
1 T Thai Kitchen. Spicy Red Chile
  Sauce
¼ C nutritional yeast flakes
1 T cumin powder
2 T sesame oil
4 cloves garlic, pressed

Oil cookie sheet. Preheat oven to 375°.

Blend half the rice and tofu in a food processor with all ingredients.

Add the remaining tofu and rice, mixing thoroughly. Form into 2" balls.

Bake for 25 minutes until golden brown.

Serve with Gombu Sauce (p. 92)

Chant: ***Gate Gate Paragate Parasamgate Bodhisvaha!***
Gone, gone, gone beyond the beyond

Prajna-paramita, Shakayamuni the Buddha Heart Sutra

*Feel that we are eating in order to maintain strength, prolong our life and thereby be able to fulfill our aspiration of benefiting others.
In this way eating becomes part of the Mahayana Buddhist practice.*

Geshe Rubten and Geshe Dhargyey,
Advice from a Spiritual Friend

Forbidden Rice Medley

8–10 servings

5 C water
2 tsp crystal salt
1½ C Chinese purple "Forbidden" rice
1½ C quinoa or white basmati rice
1½ onion, chopped
8 cloves garlic, chopped
2" ginger, grated
1 T curry powder
1 tsp allspice powder
1 T sesame oil
1 T coconut oil

2 medium carrots, chopped
½ lb kale, finely chopped
2 medium heads broccoli, chopped
2 zucchinis, chopped
tamari to taste
10 pieces vegetarian tempeh "bacon,"
   lightly sautéed in oil.

Thoroughly wash quinoa or w. Basmati by vigorously massaging and rinsing them 3-4 times. (Forbidden rice rinse just once.)

Bring water to boil in a 4 quart covered pot and add grains. Return to boil, then reduce heat on low until done, about 25 minutes.

Sauté onions, garlic, ginger, curry and allspice in oil for 5 minutes. Add carrots and kale, sauté for a few more minutes. Add broccoli and zucchini and sauté until tender.

Mix veggies and tempeh bacon with grains. Add tamari to taste.

A delicious variation is to top with Coconut, Cinnamon Squash or Yam (p. 114).

Serve with Secret Sauce (p. 95)

What is man without the beasts? If all the beasts were gone, many would die from a great loneliness of spirit. For whatever happens to the beasts soon happens to man. All things are connected.

Chief Seattle's Address, 1854

Indian Dahl

6 servings

1 T sesame oil
1 T coconut oil
1 onion, chopped
4 cloves garlic

1" ginger, peeled and chopped
2 stalks celery, chopped
1 tsp cumin powder
½ tsp Garam Masala powder

Sauté above ingredients in a 2 quart pan until onions become translucent.

1 C yellow or red lentils (may be
   soaked 4 hours, then rinsed)
1 medium potato, peeled and finely
   chopped
1 carrot, chopped
3 C water
2 tsp crystal salt
1 tsp turmeric

Wash lentils. Add water to sauté pan, bring to a boil and simmer all ingredients until water has evaporated and lentils are soft (40 min).

A traditional favorite and staple of India.

Excellent served over Basmati Rice.

When our eyes are opened and our hearts purified, the work of the same divine influence unfolding the same divinity in every human heart will become manifest; and then alone shall we be in a position to claim the brotherhood of man.

The Upanishads, translated by Juan Mascaro

Indian Pilaf

6 servings

1.5 C W. Basmati rice, washed
  and drained
2 T coconut oil
1 tsp cumin seeds
1 T minced ginger
½ tsp coriander, ground
2¾ C water
1 tsp turmeric
½ tsp garam masala
½ tsp crushed red chili flakes
¼ tsp hing powder
1/2 C raisins
1/2 C cashews, chopped
½ C carrot, finely chopped
1 C frozen green peas, defrosted
1 tsp crystal salt
3 T fresh mixed herbs, minced
  (basil, cilantro, mint)

In a 2 quart pot heat oil to medium high. Add top 3 spices and sauté for 2 minutes. Add rice and sauté for 2 more minutes.

Turn heat to high, add water and next 4 spices. Bring to boil and immediately turn to low and cover.

After cooking 15 minutes, add raisins, cashews, carrots, peas and salt to top of rice mixture.

Cover and continue cooking 5 more minutes.

Turn off heat, add remaining spices, mix well, cover and let stand 5 minutes.

Stir well, then serve.

Extra delicious when accompanied with Mango Chutney (p. 81).

Hasten your evolution by proper diet, healthful living, and reverence for your body as the temple of God.

The Upanishads, translated by Juan Mascaro

Indian Tofu Broccoli
6–8 servings

2 T coconut oil
1 T sesame oil
3 onions, chopped
1½ lbs tofu, in small chunks

In a large frying pan, sauté onions and tofu in oil on medium high heat until translucent.

3 medium tomatoes, diced
1 tsp cinnamon powder
1 tsp cardamom powder
½ tsp black pepper
1" ginger, chopped fine or grated

4 cloves garlic, pressed
1 tsp Garam Masala
½ tsp chili powder
1½ tsp crystal salt

Lower heat, add above ingredients, and simmer for 3 minutes

4 T soy milk, plain

Add soy mylk. Cover pan and let simmer for 10 minutes, stirring occasionally.

2 broccoli heads, chopped

Add broccoli for 3 more minutes of cooking.

4 T lemon juice
2 T fresh cilantro, chopped
2 fresh green chilies, chopped

Turn off heat, add remaining ingredients & serve with grain of choice

---

The irony is that, in truth, our so-called health care system is really not a health care system at all. It is a disease-care system. In other words, our system does virtually nothing to prevent disease and responds only when someone becomes sick.

Dr. Terry Shintani, M.D., J.D., M.P.H., "The Hawaii Diet"

Indian Vegetable Curry
4 servings

2 T coconut oil
½ tsp mustard seed
1 tsp cumin seeds
1 onion, chopped
1 heaping tsp turmeric
1 tsp curry powder
1 C water

1 can (15 oz) coconut milk
4 C chopped mixed veggies: carrots,
    broccoli, cauliflower, green beans,
    sweet potatoes, yams, or squash,
    peas, greens, etc.)
crystal salt, to taste

Warm seed spices briefly in oil, then add onion and sauté until translucent.

Add remaining spices and veggies that take the longest time to cook (carrot, potato, squash, etc.) gradually adding the coconut milk and water. Add remaining veggies. so that dish remains warm. Slow simmer until all veggies are cooked.

Add some chopped cilantro and a pinch or two of crystal salt to taste, if desired.

This dish can be served as is or with rice.

> *If we are serious about wanting to leave our children, and their children, a habitable world, then we have to ask where our leverage lies, and where we can be most effective. There is no other single action that is as effective at saving water as eating a plant-based diet.*
>
> John Robbins, *The Food Revolution*

Khichari
6 servings

2 T safflower oil
1 T ginger, minced
1 tsp cumin seeds
1 tsp coriander seeds
1 tsp turmeric powder
¼ tsp fenugreek
¼ tsp fennel
½ tsp crushed red chili flakes
¼ tsp hing powder
4 C water
1 C basmati w. rice, washed and drained
½ C red lentils or small yellow mung dhal, cleaned and washed
2 tsp crystal salt
1 med yam, chopped small
1 medium cauliflower, chopped
1 C carrots chopped
1 C frozen peas, defrosted
Opt: ¼ C cashews, lightly chopped
    ¼ C raisins
2 T cilantro, chopped

In a 2 quart pot sauté spice seeds in oil on medium high heat for 2 minutes.

Lower heat to medium, add spice powders and cook for 2 more minutes.

Turn heat to high and add 4 C water. When water boils add rice and dahl mixture. Return to boil, add yam, cauliflower and carrots, cover and turn heat to low.

Cook for 20 minutes, add peas and Optional ingredients. Cover and cook 5 more minutes.

Add cilantro, mix well and let stand covered for 5 more minutes before serving.

For a nutritious change use ½ C washed quinoa in place of ½ C rice

"The Great Turning" is a name for the essential adventure of our time: the shift from the industrial growth society to a life-sustaining civilization.

www.Joannamacy.net

Non-injury—Ahimsa:
"The avoidance of harm to any living creatures in thought or deed....
Do unto others as you would have them do unto you."

Mahatma Gandhi

Krishna Cakes
about 4 Divine servings

3 medium garnet yams, peeled, chopped, steamed and mashed

½ C sunflower seeds and cashews, finely chopped.

¼ C flaked coconut

1 T ginger, finely minced

½ tsp jalapeño pepper powder

1 tsp cumin powder

2 tsp coriander powder

1 tsp cinnamon powder

½ tsp nutmeg powder

1 T maple syrup

1½ T tamari or w. miso

½ C chickpea flour

¼ C sunflower or coconut oil

Opt: ¼ C red onion, minced

Preheat oven to 375°

Finely chop sunflowers and cashews in a food processor.

Mix all ingredients and divide into 12 small patties about ½" thick.

Place on a well oiled cookie sheet and bake for 20 minutes.

Flip and bake for another 15 minutes or until outside is golden brown.

Let cool and serve. Divinely Delicious!

The greatest revolution of our time is in the way we see the world. The mechanistic paradigm underlying the Industrial Growth Society gives way to the realization that we belong to a living, self-organizing cosmos. General systems theory, emerging from the life sciences, brings fresh evidence to confirm ancient, indigenous teachings: the Earth is alive, mind is pervasive, all beings are our relations. This realization changes everything. It changes our perceptions of who we are and what we need, and how we can trustfully act together for a decent, noble future.

www.Joannamacy.net

Ma Ma Mia Spanish Casserole
8-10 servings

4 C cooked brown rice or
  Forbidden rice/quinoa mix
1 C green beans, chopped & steamed
1 zucchini, chopped & steamed

2 T olive oil
1 onion, finely chopped
8 cloves garlic, finely chopped
2 T tamari
1 red bell pepper, finely chopped
4 med tomatoes chopped
1 T organic taco seasoning
1 tsp red chili pepper
1 tsp crystal salt
½ tsp black pepper
1 can "Eden Black Beans," drained
  or 1 block cooked Simply Delicious
  Tempeh (p. 140) broken into bits
4 corn tortillas, lightly steamed 1 min.

Topping
1½ batches Tofu Sour Cream (p. 83)
1 T olive oil
4 small red potatoes, chopped &
  steamed
2 T cilantro, finely chopped
1 tsp Thai Kitchen Spicy Chile Sauce

Add first three ingredients together

In a sauté pan on medium high heat add oil, onion and garlic. Cook until onions first start to become tender then add rest of ingredients. Bring to a simmer and cook for 5 minutes.

Combine with top ingredients in a mixing bowl.

Preheat oven to 375° degrees.

Combine topping ingredients and mix well in a food processor.

Add ⅓ topping to rice mixture, mix well and place ½ in an oiled 8½ x 11 baking dish. Cut steamed tortillas in eighths and spread evenly over mixture. Add remaining rice and spread rest of topping evenly over it.

Bake for 30 minutes, until top is golden and puffs up a bit.

Masala Tempeh

An exotic and spicy dish. Serves 6 to 8

1 tsp curry powder
¼ tsp mustard seeds
¼ tsp fennel seeds
¼ tsp onion seeds
¼ tsp crushed red chilies
½ tsp cumin seeds

¼ tsp fenugreek seeds
1 tsp coriander, ground
1 tsp crystal salt
1 T ginger, finely chopped
4 garlic cloves, chopped

Mix above spices together in a bowl.

2 T grape seed oil
2 T coconut oil
2 medium onions, sliced
2 medium tomatoes, chopped
12 oz green peas, frozen
2 blocks Simply Delicious
   Tempeh (p. 140)
2 T fresh cilantro, to garnish

Heat oil in a large frying pan to medium high heat, add spices, and sauté for 2 minutes.

Add onion and sauté for another few minutes.

Mix occasionally, until onions are translucent.

Add tomato and peas and cook for 3 more minutes. Cut Simply Delicious Tempeh into 8 thick slices. Add to dish, taking care to keep tempeh whole. Allow flavors to meld. Garnish and serve.

Mona's Mock Chicken Tofu

4 + servings

1 lb firm tofu block
6 T olive oil
2 T tamari
6 cloves garlic, finely chopped
1 C nutritional yeast
1 T Simply Organic All Purpose
   seasoning
1 T fresh thyme, finely chopped
½ tsp sage powder
1 tsp rosemary, finely chopped

Preheat oven to 375°. Cut tofu into ½" slices and set aside. Mix next three ingredients together and pour onto a plate.

Mix remaining ingredients together in a separate dish. Coat tofu slices with wet mixture, then lightly coat in dry mixture.

Place tofu slices in lightly oiled baking dish, sprinkling any remaining dry mixture over the top.

Bake for 30-45 minutes, until edges are crispy.

Quinoa Black Bean Enchiladas by Linda Bong
8 servings

1½ C quinoa, already cooked
5 cloves garlic, chopped
½ medium onion, chopped
½ C cilantro, chopped
3 Anaheim chilies, and 4 red
   peppers, roasted and chopped
1 tsp cumin powder
¼ tsp cayenne pepper
1 tsp crystal salt
1 chayote peeled and grated
1 block tofu, pressed dry
1 15 oz can black beans
⅛ C extra virgin olive oil
10 corn tortillas

Puree roasted peppers with herbs and a little water and put ¼ aside.
Mash tofu and mix together with quinoa, black beans, larger amount of pepper mixture and all other ingredients except tortillas and oil.
Lightly rub tortillas with water and warm in a skillet (iron preferred.)
Dip tortillas in olive oil, fill and roll allowing enough mixture for 10 tortillas.
Place in large glass baking dish, drizzle with remaining sauce and bake at 350° for 40 min.

A great dish from Linda's delightful store, deli and gift shop in South Kona.

Simply Delicious Tempeh
2–4 servings

8 oz block of tempeh
2 T safflower or
   grape seed oil
1 T sesame oil
2" ginger, finely chopped
1 T tamari

Boil tempeh whole in water for 5 minutes.
Heat oil to medium-high in a sauté pan. Add the block of tempeh and sauté for 5 minutes, until well browned and crispy. Poke holes in top with fork and pour or brush tamari over the top and flip over. At same time, add ginger to the pan alongside the tempeh and cook both for 5 more minutes or until tempeh is browned and a little crispy.
Remove tempeh from pan and slice into 6 strips. Sprinkle ginger on top and serve.

Sesame Butternut Curry
6 servings

1 medium butternut squash baked, skin removed and deseeded.
1 T safflower oil
1 T sesame oil
1 med. onion, chopped
2 T minced ginger
1 tsp cumin, fresh ground
1 tsp curry powder
½ tsp turmeric powder
2 tsp crystal salt

½ red pepper, finely chopped
2 C water
½ C sesame paste, (tahini)
½ C green beans, chopped, steamed
2 carrots, chopped, steamed
1 med. cauliflower, chopped, steamed
1 zucchini chopped, steamed
¼ C cilantro, finely chopped

Sauté onion and ginger in oil for a few minutes. Add spices, salt and red pepper and continue sauté until onions are translucent. Add water, squash, tahini and mix well. Bring to a simmer, add vegetables and cilantro and turn off heat.

Spicy Indian Rice
6 servings

2 C white basmati rice
6 cardamom pods
4 T coconut oil
1 bay leaf
2 cinnamon sticks
1 tsp crystal salt
½ C raisins

3 C water
½ C almonds, slivered

Rinse and drain the rice a few times. In a medium saucepan, sauté cardamom in oil, on med-high heat, for 1 minute.

Add all ingredients except water and almonds. Stir fry for 1 minute.

Add water, bring to a boil, reduce heat, cover, and cook on low for 20 minutes.

Stir in almonds and let stand for 5 minutes, before serving.

Sushi Rice

Makes 4 cups

2 C Japanese sushi rice, (or short grain rice) cleaned and cooked according to directions
2 T rice syrup or agave nectar
3 T rice vinegar
½ tsp crystal salt

Let cooked rice sit covered for 10 minutes.

Heat the rice syrup, vinegar and salt in a small saucepan until salt is dissolved.

Put the rice in a large mixing bowl and stir in mixture.

Allow mixture to cool.

Sushi with Avocado, Cucumber and Carrot

makes 6–8 rolls

1 cucumber, peeled
2 carrots, finely grated
1 medium avocado
1 T tamari
8 sheets nori seaweed, toasted
¼ C pickled ginger
tamari
wasabi powder paste

Cut cucumber in half lengthwise, scoop out seeds, and cut into ¼″ strips. Slice avocado into ½″ wide slices. Place a sheet of nori, shiny side down, on a bamboo mat. Using a damp spoon to prevent sticking, cover ⅔ of the sheet with rice. Add cucumber, carrot, ginger and avocado to the center of rice.

Dampen the far end of the sheet with tamari and roll away from you, using the mat to tighten the roll. With a wet knife, cut sushi into 1″ pieces.

Serve with small bowls of tamari, wasabi and more pickled ginger.
Other vegetables, tofu, etc. may be added to the sushi.
There are infinite variations on this versatile dish, including using other more nutritious grain mixtures that may not be as sticky.

Thai Coconut, Lemongrass, Kabocha Vegetable Curry

8–10 servings

1 Kabocha squash (3–4 lbs)
4–5" stalks lemongrass
2 C water
1 large onion, chopped
1 T sesame oil
1 T coconut oil
2 tsp curry powder
1 T cumin
3 T finely grated ginger
1 tsp Mae Ploy yellow curry
   paste or a bit less of Thai
   Kitchen green curry paste
1 mild red pepper
Opt: zest 1 Kefir or other lime
2 cans coconut milk
½ lb kale, finely chopped
½ lb green beans, in 1" pieces
1 head broccoli, chopped
½ C Westbrae Brown Rice
   Miso
½ C chopped cilantro

Bake squash whole in a baking dish at 375° until tender (45–60 minutes). Let cool, cut off the top, remove seeds with a fork, peel skin, and chop.

Boil lemongrass in 2 C water for 20 minutes and set aside.

Sauté onion and ginger in oil in a 3 quart pot on medium high heat. When close to done add curry paste, powder, cumin, lime zest and red pepper.

Sauté for a couple of minutes, then add coconut milk and bring to a simmer for a minute or two. Add Kabocha squash and mash a bit to thicken.

Steam kale and green beans together for 8 minutes, then add broccoli and steam for a few more minutes until just cooked, then add to the curry.

Blend lemongrass water with miso, and return to pot and mix well. Add water salt or spice, if needed, for desired consistency and taste. Gently warm, being careful not to boil miso or overcook vegetables.

Serve over jasmine or Forbidden Rice with a garnish of cilantro.

But those who know the secret of nature, those who see everywhere in nature the Oneness that is beyond nature, they alone enjoy Eternal Bliss.

♥ Pathways to Joy, Swami Vivekenanda

Wild Rice Medley

8 servings

1 C Lundberg Wild Rice Blend
  + 2 C water
½ C wild rice + 2 C water
2 T grape seed oil
2 onions, chopped
6 cloves garlic, chopped
2 carrots, thinly sliced, diagonally
2 T tamari
¼ lb green beans tipped and
  cut in 2" pieces
½ C mushrooms, sliced
1 large zucchini, in bite size pieces
1 head broccoli, chopped
¼ C water
½ C chopped walnuts
½ C sun dried tomatoes, chopped
1 tsp pepper
2 T mixed fresh parsley, rosemary
  sage and thyme leaves, chopped

In 2 separate pots, bring different rice and waters to a boil. Turn heat to low, cover and cook the rice blend for 45 minutes and the wild rice for about an hour.

Heat oil in a large sauté pan on medium high heat, then add onions and garlic.

As onions soften, add tamari, carrots and any other longer cooking vegetables.

Add veggies according to cooking times, adding faster cooking vegetables such as broccoli last. Add water as needed

Add walnuts, tomatoes and spices at end when veggies are just about tender and cook for a short time longer.

Combine vegetables with the cooked rice medley in a large bowl and mix well.

Opt: Accent beautifully with Coconut, Cinnamon Squash or Yam (p. 114).

In our time, there is an awakening sense of compassion toward animals. We can run from it. We can deny it. We can mock those who stand for it. But when we choose to eat with conscience, I truly believe that our world becomes a kinder and safer place for us all.

John Robbins, *The Food Revolution*

Zucchini Love Boats
6 servings

2 C cooked Quinoa

Baked Veggies
1 small yellow onion,
5 cloves garlic
1 small globe eggplant
1 medium red bell pepper

Seasonings
¼ C nutritional yeast flakes
3 T raw or roasted tahini
2 T fresh lemon juice
2 T tamari

Zucchini Boats
3 large zucchini, cut in half
   lengthwise and steamed until
   almost tender, about 5 minutes

Preheat the oven to 400° F.

Baked Veggies: On a baking sheet lined with kitchen parchment paper, put the whole and unpeeled onion, garlic, eggplant, and bell pepper. Bake at 400° F for 15 minutes. Remove the garlic, turn the other vegetables and return them to the oven. Continue baking until the onion and eggplant are tender and the pepper is blistered and slightly blackened, about 15 more minutes. When cool enough to handle, remove and discard the skin from the onion and garlic. Remove the skin, stem and seeds from the bell pepper. Cut all the Baked Veggies into large pieces.

When the Zucchini Boats are cool enough to handle, scrape out the center of each zucchini. Discard the pulp and save the shells for stuffing.

In a food processor, put the Baked Veggies and all the ingredients under Seasonings. Pulse until chopped small. Stop the food processor, add the cooked quinoa and pulse several more times to mix.

Put an oven rack about 2 inches below the broiler. Preheat the broiler with the door closed. Lightly oil a baking sheet or line with kitchen parchment paper.

Fill each hollowed out zucchini with the quinoa mixture and put it on the prepared baking sheet. Broil until a light golden color on top, about 5 minutes. Keep a watchful eye on your zucchini boats so they do not burn.

Serve with Walnut Sage Sauce (p. 98).

 # Desserts

~ Cookies ~

Apricot Dreams (Raw)
makes about 20 dreams

1 C raw almonds, soaked 6 hours
1 C dried apricots, soaked 2 hours
½ C pitted dates, soaked 1 hour
½ C raisins
1 T grated lemon peel

Drain all soaked items. Save soak water for smoothies. Grind almonds, apricots and dates in a food processor. Mix in raisins and grated lemon and form into small cookies or balls. Store in the refrigerator.

Bliss Balls (Raw)
about 10 blisses

½ C dates, soaked
4 T hemp seeds
2 T bee pollen
2 T raw cacao powder
4 T coconut flakes
½ C ground nuts
½ tsp cardamom
½ tsp cinnamon

Chop dates and soak for half an hour in just enough liquid (¼ C) to cover.

Process nuts of choice in a food processor, into a semi-fine meal with some chunks.

Mix all ingredients together and roll into 1" balls.

Refrigerate for 1 hour and serve.

Stores well in the freezer for extended periods.

Opt: 2 tsp spirulina and/or 2 tsp cacao nibs
More liquid may be added and batter shaped into bars and dehydrated!

Carob Cookies
about 10 cookies

1 C chopped figs
¼ C pitted dates
1 C mac nuts
¼ C carob powder
1 tsp ground cinnamon
½ C coconut flakes

Soak figs and dates in water for 1 hour, then drain. Grind all ingredients except coconut flakes in a food processor until smooth.

Refrigerate for a few hours then form into balls. Roll in coconut. Store in refrigerator.

Chocolate Macadamia Nut Cookies
16–24 cookies

1 C agave nectar
½ C safflower or grape seed oil
1 tsp vanilla extract

2 C white spelt or whole wheat flour
½ C chocolate powder
1 tsp baking powder
1 tsp baking soda
½ tsp crystal salt
½ C raw mac nuts, chopped

Combine wet ingredients and dry ingredients separately, then mix the two together into a dough.

Drop by tablespoonful an inch apart onto oiled baking sheets.

Bake at 350° for 15 minutes.

> *This we know. The Earth does not belong to man: man belongs to the Earth. This we know. All things are connected like the blood, which unites one family. All things are connected.*
>
> Chief Seattle's Address, 1854

Coconut Carrot Ginger Cookies

Makes 2½ dozen

Dry Mixture
2 C white spelt or barley flour
2 C old fashion rolled oats
1 C shredded dried coconut, unsweetened
1 C organic cane sugar
2 tsp baking powder
1 tsp baking soda
½ tsp crystal salt
1 C currants or chocolate chips

Wet Mixture
½ C coconut or grape seed oil
½ C apple or orange juice
2 T finely grated fresh ginger
2 tsp pure vanilla extract
1 C grated carrot

Preheat the oven to 350º F. Line a baking sheet with kitchen parchment paper or spread ¼ C shredded dried coconut on an un-oiled baking sheet. The coconut will give your cookies a nice bottom crust and prevent them from sticking.

Dry Mixture: In a large bowl, put all the Dry Mixture and whisk together.

Wet Mixture: In a medium bowl, put all the Wet Mixture and stir together.

Pour the Wet Mixture over the Dry Mixture and stir together.

Drop rounded teaspoons of dough, 1-inch apart, onto the prepared baking sheet.

Bake at 350° F until the edges are a light golden color, about 15 minutes. Do not over-bake as the cookies will continue to cook on the hot baking sheet after they are removed from the oven. Let the cookies cool 10 minutes before removing them from the baking sheet. Do not stack cookies until they are completely cool as they will stick together.

Coconut Ginger Oatmeal Bars
Makes 20 two-inch square bars

Dry Mixture
1½ C spelt or barley flour
1 C old fashion rolled oats
1 C shredded dry coconut
1 C goji berries or chocolate chips
½ C coarsely chopped mac nuts

¾ C Rapidura (sweetener)
1½ tsp cinnamon powder
1½ tsp ginger powder
1 tsp baking powder
1 tsp baking soda
½ tsp crystal salt

Wet Mixture
½ cup coconut or grape seed oil
¾ cup orange juice
1 T finely grated orange rind

Preheat the oven to 350° F. Oil a
9 x 9-inch glass baking dish.

Dry Mixture: In a large bowl, put all the Dry Mixture and whisk together.

Wet Mixture: In a medium bowl, put all the Wet Mixture and stir together.

Pour the Wet Mixture in with the Dry Mixture and stir to mix. Spoon the cookie dough into the oiled baking dish and spread evenly.

Bake at 350° F until the cookies are firm to the touch and a golden color on top, about 30 minutes.

Let cool 20 minutes before cutting into squares.

Before storing cookies, make sure they are completely cool. Store cut cookies in an air-tight container with sheets of wax paper between the layers. These cookies will keep about a week if stored properly.

Ginger Cookies
makes 24 cookies

¾ C maple syrup
¼ C unsulphured molasses
½ C coconut oil, melted
¼ C fresh ginger root, grated

2½ C white spelt or barley flour
1 tsp baking powder
1 tsp baking soda
½ tsp crystal salt
1 tsp cinnamon
¼ tsp allspice

Blend first 3 ingredients together.

Mix in ginger.

Mix dry ingredients together.

Combine wet and dry ingredients, mixing well.

Drop by tablespoonful onto oiled baking sheets 1 inch apart.

Bake at 350° for 10-15 minutes.

Indescribably delicious with a topping of Artemesa raw coconut butter

Molasses cookies
makes 16-24

¾ C grape seed or coconut oil
1 C molasses
1 C rolled oats
2 C white spelt or oat flour

1 tsp vanilla extract
1 tsp cinnamon powder
1 tsp crystal salt

Mix oil molasses and rest of ingredients and blend well. Separate into 2 even batches and drop spoonfuls on 2 oiled cookie sheets.

Bake till golden brown, 15 –20 minutes

Prasad

Makes 108 1-inch Squares.

Dry Mixture
1 C cacao nibs
1 C raw mac nuts or cashews
1 C raw Brazil nuts
½ C raw white sesame seeds
½ C Goji berries
1 tsp cinnamon powder
¼ tsp crystal salt

Wet Mixture
½ C agave nectar
½ C cacao butter, melted

Note: Nuts, seeds and berries should be at room temperature.

Dry & Wet Mixtures: In a food processor, with the S shaped blade, put all the Dry Mixture and process until it stops flowing through blades. Continue to process while adding the Wet Mixture through the food shoot . Process until smooth. You may see small pieces of goji berries and cacao nibs.

Line the bottom of a small cookie sheet with parchment paper or wax paper. Spread the mixture evenly on top of the paper. Refrigerate until firm, about 10 minutes.

Remove Prasad from the refrigerator and cut into 1-inch squares.

Store in the refrigerator, with sheets of wax paper between the layers, for up to 3 weeks. Serve soon after removing from the refrigerator.

Oatmeal, Pineapple, Mac Nut Cookies
makes 2 dozen cookies

¼ C safflower oil
1 C maple syrup
1 tsp crystal salt
1 tsp cinnamon
1 tsp vanilla

1 ¾ C oat flour
2 ½ C oats
⅔ C dried pineapple chunks
¾ C mac nuts or walnuts, chopped

Preheat oven to 375°. Mix all ingredients together into a batter. Drop by tablespoonful onto a lightly oiled cookie sheet. Bake for 15-17 minutes at 375°. Please note: these cookies do not turn brown when done.

Super Delicious Cookies
2 dozen cookies

1 C sunflower or safflower oil
1 C maple syrup
1 C raw tahini
2 tsp vanilla
2 ½ C rolled oats
3 C white spelt flour
or 2 C white spelt + 1 C oat flour
½ C almonds, chopped, or
   white sesame seeds, whole
2 tsp baking soda
½ tsp crystal salt

Mix wet ingredients together well in a medium bowl.

Mix dry ingredients together well.

Add dry ingredients to wet and mix together in a large bowl.

Bake on an oiled cookie sheets for 15 minutes at 350°.

Opt: ½ C dark or semi-sweet chocolate chips (Sunspire Brand)

Tahini Sesame Cookies

Makes 2 dozen cookies

Dry Mixture
2 C white spelt or barley flour
½ C raw sesame seeds
1 tsp baking powder
1 tsp baking soda
½ tsp crystal salt

Wet Mixture
1 C agave nectar or pure maple syrup
1 C raw tahini (sesame butter)
¼ C coconut or grape seed oil
2 tsp pure vanilla extract

Preheat oven to 350 F. Line 2 baking sheets with kitchen parchment paper or lightly oil them and evenly spread ¼ cup sesame seeds over each baking sheet. The sesame seeds will give a nice bottom crust to your cookies and keep them from sticking to the pans.

Dry Mixture: In a large bowl, put all the Dry Mixture and whisk together.

Wet Mixture: In a blender, put all the Wet Mixture and blend until smooth.

Pour the Wet Mixture over the Dry Mixture and stir together.

Roll 1 tablespoon of the dough into a ball and put it on the prepared baking sheet. Press your thumb down on the center of the ball of dough to flatten it. Repeat with the remaining dough, putting each ball of dough 1 inch apart on the baking sheets.

Bake at 350° F until done, about 14 minutes. Let cool for 10 minutes before removing from the baking sheets.

> *If most health issues are caused by dietary excesses (and they are), then it makes sense that the subtraction of such excesses is likely to be an effective treatment strategy.*
>
> Douglas J. Lisle, Ph.D., & Alan Goldhammer, D.C., *The Pleasure Trap*

Temple Bliss Balls
Makes 36 1-inch balls

Sunflower Meal
½ C raw sunflower seeds or coconut
   flakes

Almond Paste
2 C (about 1 jar) roasted almond butter
   or roasted hazelnut butter
¼ C carob powder or cacao powder
¼ C pure maple syrup or agave nectar
6 dates, pits removed and soaked in
   ¼ cup water for 3 hours
1 tsp cinnamon powder
1 tsp pure vanilla extract
½ C currants, dried cranberries
Opt: ¼ C cacao nibs

Sunflower Meal
In a food processor, with the S-shaped blade, add the sunflower seeds or coconut flakes and process until a crumbly meal. Put in a bowl and set aside.

In a food processor, with the S-shaped blade, combine all the ingredients, except the currants, dried cranberries or cacao nibs. Process into a thick paste. Stop the food processor and add remaining ingredients as specified to the left.

Take 1 T of the almond paste and shape it into a ball. Roll the ball in the sunflower meal or coconut and put it onto a large platter. Repeat with the remaining almond paste.

Serve as is or freeze first. If freezing, serve soon after removing them from the freezer as they will thaw quickly.

Store in a covered glass container in the refrigerator for up to a month or in the freezer for up to 2 months.

Muffins & Breads

Babaji Bread
8 servings

1½ C white spelt flour
1½ C oat flour
½ tsp Himalayan crystal salt
2 tsp baking powder
½ tsp baking soda
1 tsp cardamom powder
1 tsp cinnamon powder
½ tsp nutmeg powder
¼ tsp clove powder
½ C Himalayan goji berries
¾ C manuka raisins
½ C tofu blended well with
　¾ C water
⅔ C agave nectar
½ C raw coconut oil, melted

Preheat oven to 350°.

Combine, flour, salt, baking soda and spices in a bowl.

Add all liquid ingredients to a blender or food processor and lightly blend or pulse with raisins and gogi berries.

Pour liquid ingredients into dry mixture and combine well.

Spread mixture into a lightly oiled 4" x 8" bread pan. Bake for 45 minutes.

Let fully cool and add a light frosting of Artemesa coconut butter when serving!

Truth, Simplicity, Love, Service to Humanity and Chanting God's Name. Om Namah Shivaya....

Hadakhan Babaji   www.Babaji.net

155

Banana Walnut Bread

Makes 8 servings

Dry Mixture
2 C white spelt or barley flour
2 T roasted grain beverage
  (coffee substitute like Inka)
1 tsp baking powder
1 tsp baking soda
½ tsp crystal salt
1 C chopped walnuts, soaked 3 hours

Wet Mixture
1 ripe banana, cut large
1 C vanilla rice beverage or soy milk
½ C Rapidura (sweetener)
½ C coconut or grape seed oil
1 ripe banana, sliced
1 T finely grated fresh ginger

Preheat oven to 350º. Lightly oil an 8 x 8-inch glass baking dish and dust with flour or to make muffins, line 2 muffin pans with paper muffin liners.

Dry Mixture: In a large bowl, put all the Dry Mixture and stir together.

Wet Mixture: In a blender, put all the Wet Mixture, except the sliced banana and ginger, and blend until smooth. Stop the blender, add the sliced banana and grated ginger and stir to mix..

Pour the Wet Mixture over the Dry Mixture and stir together.

Pour the batter into the oiled baking dish or muffin pans and shake to make it level.

Bake at 350º until the bread is done, about 40 minutes for bread and 30 minutes for muffins.

Let cool for 10 minutes before cutting and removing from baking dish.

Banana + Muffins
12 muffins

1 C pitted dates, soaked 30 minutes
2 C bananas, mashed or cooked
   squash or apple sauce
2 T coconut or safflower oil
1 tsp vanilla
1 tsp cinnamon
½ tsp nutmeg
¼ tsp clove
2 C oat flour
1 tsp baking powder
½ tsp baking soda
1 tsp crystal salt

Preheat oven to 425°.
Blend dates with just enough soak water to cover them.
Mix wet ingredients and spices together with blended dates in a bowl.
Mix dry ingredients in a separate bowl.
Mix well wet ingredients to dry.
Pour batter into oiled muffin tins and bake at 425° for 15 minutes and 350° for 25 minutes. Check with a toothpick to see if it comes out clean.
Opt: 1 C chopped nuts or chocolate chips.

Carrot Bread Supreme
Makes 2 loaves

4 C carrots, grated
¼ C lemon juice
1 C safflower oil
1 C agave nectar
¾ C raisins
¾ C nuts, chopped
4 C white spelt flour
Opt: ¼ C carrot juice

1 tsp vanilla
1 tsp crystal salt
½ tsp nutmeg
1½ tsp cinnamon
4 tsp baking powder
1 tsp baking soda
4 C white spelt flour

Mix all ingredients together and add to 2 standard pastry loaf baking pans.
Bake at 350° for 1 hour. Allow to cool.

Pineapple Date Muffins
Makes 1 dozen muffins

Dry Mixture
2 C white spelt or barley flour
1 C coarsely chopped raw mac nuts
1 tsp baking powder
1 tsp baking soda
1 tsp cinnamon powder
½ tsp crystal salt

Wet Mixture
1 C fresh or canned crushed unsweetened pineapple, drained
¾ C pineapple juice or apple juice
½ C agave nectar or pure maple syrup
½ C chopped small dates
¼ C coconut or grape seed oil
1 tsp pure vanilla extract

Preheat the oven to 350°. Line 2 muffin pans with paper muffin cups.

Dry Mixture: In a large mixing bowl, put all the Dry Mixture and stir together.

Wet Mixture: In a small bowl, put all the Wet Mixture and stir together.

Pour the Wet Mixture over the Dry Mixture and stir together..

In the prepared muffin pan, fill each cup ¾ full with the batter.

Bake at 350° until the muffins are done, about 30 minutes.

Let the muffins cool for 10 minutes before removing them from the pan.

Zucchini Muffins

Makes 1 dozen of the best muffins ever!

3 C flour (oat, spelt, whole
   wheat pastry combo)
½ tsp crystal salt
1 tsp baking powder
½ tsp baking soda
1 tsp nutmeg
1 T cinnamon

2 C zucchini, grated (with skins on)
½ C safflower oil
⅔ C Sucanat
4 T agave nectar
1 T vanilla
1 C applesauce
Flax egg replacer for 2 eggs (p. 18)

Optional: 1 C chopped nuts (walnut, macadamia nut, pecan, sunflower seeds)

Preheat oven to 350°. Sift dry ingredients together. Mix wet ingredients together separately. Fold in nuts, if desired. Use oiled muffin tin or line with paper muffin cups. Bake at 325° for 25-30 minutes or until cooked in the middle.

> *Diane Courtney, head of the Toxic Effects Branch of the EPA's National Environmental Research Center, told Congress that "dioxin is by far the most toxic chemical known to mankind. Dioxin is obviously not a substance you'd want on your plants. Yet the EPA says that up to 95 percent of human dioxin exposure comes from red meat, fish, and dairy products."*
>
> John Robbins, *The Food Revolution*

Puddings & Crisps

Apple Bake
4 servings

4 apples, cored and top peeled
¼ C raisins
½ C mixed dates, prunes, apricots and
   cherries, chopped
¼ C walnuts, chopped
1 T maple syrup
2 tsp allspice powder
1 T grated ginger
⅛ tsp clove powder
1 lemon, juiced

Preheat oven to 375°

Place apples in a square glass baking
dish with ¼" of water in bottom.
Add all ingredients to a bowl and mix
well.
Stuff cored apples with mixture
placing any extra in baking dish.
Bake for 1 hour until apples are well
done, almost mushy.

Serve with Soy Delicious vanilla ice cream topped with extra fruit and nut mix.

Apple Cherry Crisp
8 servings

6 green apples, peeled and sliced
2 C frozen pitted cherries, halved
¼ C maple syrup
3 T white spelt flour

4 T apple juice
1 T fresh lemon juice
1 tsp cinnamon
½ tsp ground allspice

Preheat oven to 375°
Mix above ingredients together in a bowl and pour into a 9 x 13" baking dish

½ C raw walnuts or
   mac nuts, chopped
1 C white spelt flour
2 C rolled oats
½ C grape seed oil
½ C maple syrup
2 tsp cinnamon

Rough grind nuts in a food processor.

Mix all ingredients together in a bowl and
evenly distribute over the apple mixture.

Bake for 30 to 35 minutes or until bubbling
and lightly browned. Cool before serving.

Apricot Rice Pudding
Makes 3½ cups

2 C leftover cooked brown rice
½ C dried apricots, in small pieces
½ C coconut flakes
½ C raisins or currants
6 dates, pits removed
2 C nut or seed mylk (p. 47)

2 tsp pure vanilla extract
1 tsp cinnamon powder
1 tsp ginger powder
1 tsp cardamom powder
½ tsp turmeric powder
½ tsp crystal salt

Decoration, Optional
½ C almonds, blanched and skins removed. slivered.

In medium saucepan, put all ingredients and simmer until thick, about 5 minutes.

Pour the rice pudding into a large serving bowl or into individual dessert bowls. Arrange the almonds in a decorative pattern on the top(s) of the pudding and then lightly dust with cinnamon powder.

Let cool and then refrigerate for at least 1 hour before serving.

> *There is a social myth that a life without meat and dairy is difficult, prone to malnutrition, and void of satisfaction and texture. On the contrary, I've found that the healthier my eating habits have become, the more flavors and culinary joys I have discovered. I am now in better physical health than I have ever been, with more stamina and zest for life.*
>
> John Robbins, *The Food Revolution*

Ginger Plum Cobbler

Makes one 8 x 8-inch cobbler

Filling
8 plums, pits removed and
    sliced thin (about 5 cups)
⅓ C agave nectar or other sweetener
¼ C frozen orange juice concentrate
2 T instant tapioca
    or arrowroot powder
1 T finely grated fresh ginger
1 tsp cinnamon powder
½ tsp cardamom powder

Crust - Dry Mixture
1 C white spelt or barley flour
1 C old fashioned rolled oats
½ C shredded dried coconut,
unsweetened
1½ tsp baking powder
½ tsp crystal salt

Crust - Wet Mixture
½ C Rapidura (sweetener)
⅓ C coconut oil, melted
⅓ C orange or apple juice

Preheat oven to 350º.

Filling: In an 8 x 8-inch glass baking dish, put all the ingredients for the Filling and stir to mix.

Crust - Dry Mixture: In a medium bowl, put all the ingredients for the Crust - Dry Mixture and whisk together.

Crust - Wet Mixture: In a small bowl, put all the Crust - Wet Mixture ingredients and stir together.

Pour the Wet Mixture over the Dry Mixture and stir together.

Spread the crust mixture over the Filling and spread evenly. Bake at 350° until golden on top and bubbly inside, about 35 minutes.

Indian Rice Pudding
4–6 servings

3 C soy milk
¼ C maple syrup or agave nectar
1 tsp cinnamon powder
1 tsp cardamom powder
½ C raisins or other dried fruit, chopped
1 T finely grated ginger
4 T agar agar flakes
1 T vanilla extract
2 C short grain brown rice, cooked
¼ C almonds, slivered
2 T toasted coconut flakes

Bring soy milk to a boil.

Whisk in all ingredients listed above rice and keep at a rolling simmer for 5 minutes, whisking often.

Lightly blend 1 cup of rice with half of the soy milk mixture.

Pour all ingredients into a small baking dish, mix well, and let cool and solidify.

Sprinkle almonds and coconut flakes on top.

Serve with Mango Coconut Cream Sauce (p. 173).

Jell-O—Vegan Style
8 servings

1 T arrowroot powder
½ C fruit juice

2 C fruit juice
2 T agar agar flakes
2 C fruit
Opt: ½ tsp almond extract
1 T maple syrup

Dissolve arrowroot powder in ½ C fruit juice and set aside. In a medium pot, bring the remaining fruit juice to a boil, add agar agar flakes and half of the fruit and simmer on a low boil for 5 or so minutes, stirring frequently.

Add arrowroot and juice mixture, continue stirring and cooking, then turn off as soon as bubbles appear.

Add the remaining fruit and pour in a shallow glass baking dish. Refrigerate until solidified (1-2 hours).

Top with nut cream sauce (p. 174) for a tempting and healthy treat!
Variations: apple juice / strawberries, peach juice / peaches, grape juice / grapes...

Mango Delight
6 servings

1 T arrowroot powder
2½ C soy milk, vanilla or original
2 T agar agar flakes
2 C mango, in chunks

½ tsp vanilla
1 tsp cardamom, ground
4 T agave or maple syrup

Dissolve arrowroot powder in ½ C soy milk and set aside.
Bring remaining soy milk to a boil in a medium pot.
Add agar agar and mango.
Simmer for 5 minutes, stirring frequently. Add arrowroot mixture, return to a simmer, then remove from heat immediately. Pour into a shallow glass baking dish *or* into a Raw Pie Crust (p. 179). Refrigerate until hardened (1-2 hours).

"Ma" Freedom's Ginger Vanilla Chai Cacao Dreams

¾ C hemp seeds
¼ C coconut butter
¼ C raw coconut oil
½ C agave nectar
1 C gogi berry soak mylk =
  1 C gogi berries soaked 2
  hours in 2 C sesame mylk
¾ C raw cacao powder

1 T maca Powder
1" peeled ginger, finely grated
1 tsp cinnamon
1 tsp vanilla powder or 2 tsp vanilla
  essence
½ tsp cardamom powder
½ tsp Garam masala
¼ tsp clove powder

Put all ingredients in a blender and blend well. Pour into small cups or glass dish and refrigerate or freeze. May be used as a sauce or frosting.
With gratitude to the esteemed Raw Cacao Goddess herself, Freedom!

Cheryl's Creamy Dreamy Coconut Vanilla Tapioca Pudding
9–12 servings

1 C tapioca pearls
4 C organic coconut milk
4 C water
½ to ¾ C grade b* maple
  syrup (depending upon
  desired sweetness)
¾ tsp finely ground sea salt
4 tsp pure vanilla flavor
1 tsp pumpkin pie spice
  and/or cinnamon

Mix all ingredients together by hand in a 4-qt. pot. For best results, soak overnight in fridge (minimum soak, 4 hrs).

Remove from fridge, warm slowly on medium heat, stirring continuously, slowly bringing tapioca mixture to a gentle boil. Reduce heat to low, still stirring, 'til pearls look translucent, about 5 minutes or less. Total cooking time about 20 minutes.

Enjoy warm or enjoy a couple hours after chilling in fridge.

For a delightful tropical twist, top with mango slices and/or fresh lilikoi juice. Strawberries, kiwi, peaches, apricots, or any tasty fruit are delicious to add on top of the tapioca! Be creative! Yum!

> *Another aspect of the collective dysfunction of the human mind is the unprecedented violence that humans are inflicting on other life forms and the planet itself—the destruction of oxygen producing forests and other plant and animal life; ill treatment of animals in factory farms; and poisoning of rivers, oceans, and air.*
>
> Eckhart Tolle, *A New Earth*

Tropical Fruit Crumble

12 servings

Fruit Mixture:
2 lbs mangos, chopped
1 lb papaya
Opt: ¼ C Sucanat
    zest of 1 lime

Crust:
2 C oats
1 C mac nuts, well chopped
1 C white spelt flour
1 C coconut flakes
¾ C agave nectar or maple syrup
½ C coconut or safflower oil
1 T cinnamon

Mix mangos, papayas, Sucanat and lime zest together and place in a medium sized, lightly oiled baking dish.

Preheat oven to 375°.

Grind 1 C of the oats into a rough flour, using a food processor or blender.

Mix all crust ingredients together and spread evenly over the fruit mixture.

Bake for 30 minutes.

Serve with Lillikoi Passion Sauce (p. 173).

The physical needs for food, air, water, shelter, clothing, and basic comforts could be easily met for all humans on the planet, were it not for the imbalance of resources created by the insane and rapacious need for more, the greed of the ego. It finds collective expression in the economic structures of the world, such as huge corporations, which are egoic entities that compete with each other for more. Their only blind aim is profit.

Eckhart Tolle, *A New Earth*

 # Cakes

Carrot Cake

12 or more delicious servings
A vegan delight and always a favorite.

2 C white spelt pastry flour
2 C oat flour
¾ C Rapidura (sweetener)
1 tsp baking soda
1½ tsp baking powder
½ tsp crystal salt
1 tsp pumpkin pie spice
2 tsp cinnamon, ground
½ C raisins
1½ C carrots, finely grated

2 C apple sauce
Egg replacer for 3 eggs (p. 18)
½ C pitted dates, mashed
½ C coconut or safflower oil

Opt:
1 C fresh pineapple in small chunks
½ C macadamia or walnuts, chopped

Preheat oven to 350°.

Combine first 10 ingredients, adding grated carrots at the end.

Blend remaining ingredients together and add to above dry mixture.

Mix in Optional ingredients.

Place batter in an oiled and floured 9" x 13" glass baking dish.

Bake at 350° for 40 minutes or until a toothpick inserted in the center comes out dry.

Top with your favorite icing or with Zesty Lemon Frosting (p. 176).

The best things in life aren't things.

Fig Cake (Vegan Figgy Pudding)

8 yummy servings

Wet ingredients
1½ C dried figs chopped and soaked 1
    hour in ¾ C water
½ C safflower or coconut oil, melted
½ C applesauce
¼ C molasses or maple syrup
¼ C agave nectar
½ C dried apple, chopped
2 tsp orange zest
½ C plain soy mylk

Dry ingredients
½ C walnuts, chopped
1.5 C oat flour
1 C white spelt flour
2 tsp baking powder
½ tsp baking soda
1 tsp cinnamon powder
½ tsp allspice powder
½ tsp nutmeg powder
1 tsp salt

Preheat oven to 350°.
Blend or pulse chop fig mixture lightly.
Add all wet ingredients together and in a separate bowl mix dry ingredients
thoroughly. Mix together stirring just enough to combine well. Oil a 4" x 8" bread
pan and bake for 1 hour. Let cool fully and remove from pan.
A Christmas treat that is delicious year round!

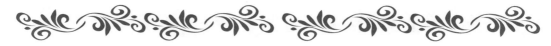

Lemon Poppy Seed Cake
Makes one 8 x 8-inch cake

Dry Mixture
2 C white spelt pastry or barley flour
1 tsp baking soda
1 tsp baking powder
½ tsp crystal salt

Wet Mixture
½ C unfiltered apple or pineapple juice
½ C agave nectar
½ C coconut oil, melted
¼ C poppy seeds

Lemon Glaze, optional
3 T rice syrup or agave nectar
3 T coconut oil, melted
3 T fresh lemon juice
2 tsp finely grated lemon rind

Preheat oven to 350º F. Lightly oil an 8 x 8-inch baking dish or a 9-inch tube pan and dust with flour.

Dry Mixture: In a medium bowl, put all the Dry Mixture and whisk together.

Wet Mixture: In a medium bowl, put all the Wet Mixture and stir together.

Pour the Wet Mixture over the Dry Mixture and stir to mix.

Pour the batter into the oiled baking dish/pan. Shake the pan to evenly spread the batter.

Bake at 350º F until the cake is done, about 40 minutes. A cake is done when the top is firm to the touch and a wooden toothpick, inserted near the center, comes out clean. Let the cake cool 20 minutes before removing it from the pan.

Lemon Glaze (optional): In a small bowl, put all the ingredients for the glaze and stir together. Pour the glaze over the top of the cake while it is still warm.

Pineapple Upside Down Cake

8 + servings

1 C pineapple juice
1 C applesauce
½ C maple syrup
¼ C safflower or sunflower oil
1 tsp pure vanilla flavor
½ C pitted dates, chopped

2 C white spelt or
    whole wheat pastry flour
1 C oat flour
2 tsp baking powder
1 tsp baking soda
2 tsp cinnamon
1 tsp pumpkin pie spice
½ tsp crystal salt
½ C raisins

1 C fresh pineapple, chopped
½ C raw mac nuts, finely chopped
4 T flaked coconut
1 T maple syrup

Preheat oven to 350°. Mix liquid ingredients and dates together in a bowl.

Whisk flours, baking powder, spices, soda and salt together in a large bowl. Stir in raisins. Add liquid ingredients to dry and combine without over-mixing.

Mix pineapple, nuts and coconut together and layer on the bottom of a medium-size glass baking dish oiled with raw coconut oil.

Pour the cake batter carefully over the bottom layer.

Bake for 30 minutes or until done.

Let cool for half an hour and gently flip cake onto a platter. Drizzle more maple syrup over the top if increased sweetness is desired.

The day that hunger is eradicated from the Earth, there will be the greatest spiritual explosion the world has ever known. Humanity cannot imagine the joy that will burst into the world on the day of that great revolution.

Federico Garcia Lorca

Pineapple Cake

12 servings

Dry Mixture
2 C white spelt or barley flour
1 tsp baking powder
1 tsp baking soda
½ tsp crystal salt

Pineapple Glaze (optional)
¼ C frozen concentrated pineapple juice
3 T coconut oil, melted
3 T agave nectar

Wet Mixture
1 C frozen concentrated pineapple juice
¾ C Rapidura (sweetener)
⅓ C coconut oil, melted
¼ C fresh lemon juice
2 tsp pure vanilla extract
2 C crushed pineapple, drained and liquid reserved

Preheat oven to 350°. Lightly oil an 8 x 8-inch baking dish or a 9-inch tube pan and dust with flour.

Dry Mixture: In a medium bowl, put all the Dry Mixture and whisk together.

Wet Mixture: In a medium bowl, put all the Wet Mixture and stir together.

Pour the Wet Mixture over the Dry Mixture and stir to mix.

Pour the batter into the oiled baking dish/pan. Shake the pan to evenly spread the batter.

Bake at 350° until the cake is done, about 40 minutes. A cake is done when the top is firm to the touch and a wooden toothpick, inserted near the center, comes out clean. Let the cake cool 20 minutes before removing it from the pan.

Pineapple Glaze (optional): In a small bowl, put all the ingredients for the glaze and stir together. Pour the glaze over the top of the cake while it is still warm.

Vegan Chocolate Cake by Amber

12 servings

3 C unbleached org. flour
⅔ C unsweetened cocoa powder
1 tsp baking soda
1 tsp crystal salt
1 tsp cinnamon
½ tsp cardamom
2 C Rapadura sweetener
1 C safflower oil
2 C chilled water or brewed
  coffee substitute
4 tsp pure vanilla
3½ T apple cider vinegar

Preheat oven to 350º. Oil 2 round cake pans.

In a large bowl sift together flour, cocoa, soda, salt and sweetener

In another bowl blend water, oil, vanilla and spices until smooth

Mix wet ingredients to dry until batter is uniform. Blend in vinegar and immediately pour into 2 baking pans.

Bake 30 to 35 minutes, cool 20 minutes

After cooling about 10 minutes, slide a knife around the edge of the cake to detach it from the pan. Invert the cake. Frost when cool with Vegan Chocolate Frosting (p. 175).

Yummy Raw Carrot Cake

12 servings

Requires the use of a champion Juicer (homogenizer)

2 C dates
1 C raisins
2 ½ C carrots, grated
1½ C coconut flakes
1 tsp nutmeg
3 tsp cinnamon
Rind of 1 lemon, grated
1 tsp ginger, grated

Soak dates and raisins in a little water for 2 hours.

Drain well, then homogenize through a champion juicer or grind well in a food processor.

Sprinkle ¼ C coconut on the bottom of a flat dish.

Put aside ¼ C of coconut for top garnish.

Mix remaining ingredients together.

Press mixture into the plate in a round cake shape.

Top with remaining coconut flakes.

Refrigerate for several hours. It will firm up nicely and can be cut into slices.
Serve with topping or dessert sauce of choice.

 # Dessert Sauces

Blueberry Sauce

4 C blueberries
¼ C Sucanat
1 C apple juice

2 T maple syrup
½ tsp allspice powder
1 tsp arrowroot powder

Cook over medium heat for 10 minutes or until thickened.

Lilikoi Passion Sauce

1 C raw mac nuts, soaked
2 T maple syrup
4 passion fruits, juiced

Place all ingredients in food processor and blend until creamy smooth. A few passion fruit seeds may be left in for crunchiness

Mango Coconut Cream Sauce

Pulp of 1 large mango
1 can coconut milk
1 tsp cardamom powder
2 T maple syrup or 4 dates

Thoroughly mix all ingredients together in a blender or food processor.
For added fun substitute an exotic fruit like sapote or a handful of goji berries.

Maple Whip

12 oz silken tofu
3 T maple syrup
1 T lemon juice

½ tsp vanilla extract
pinch cardamom
pinch cinnamon

Blend ingredients in a blender to a whipped consistency.

Strawberry Sauce

2 C strawberries, washed, hulled and sliced thin,
agave nectar or pure maple syrup, to taste

In a medium bowl, add the cut strawberries and agave nectar and stir together.
Refrigerate for at least 1 hour.

Cashew Cream
6 servings

1 C raw cashews
1½ C purified or spring water
2 T agave nectar or pure maple syrup
½ tsp vanilla
2 T coconut oil
Optional: ½ tsp nutmeg

Add all ingredients in blender with water and puree until smooth and creamy. (Add more water if needed to keep the blender mixing.)

Will keep in refrigerator for up to one week.

Coconut Sesame Cream
6 servings

1 C dehydrated coconut
1 C raw white sesame seeds
½ C dates, soaked if needed
½ tsp cardamom powder

1 tsp cinnamon powder
2 tsp vanilla extract
⅛ tsp crystal salt
3-4 C water

In a blender, put all the ingredients and blend until smooth. The finished cream will have a lot of texture to it, especially if left thick. The more water and longer it's blended, the smoother it will become.

Store in a covered glass jar in the refrigerator for up to 3 days. Shake before serving. Coconut Sesame Cream can be frozen for up to a month. Thaw at room temperature before serving.

Raspberry Carob Sauce
Makes 1 cup

¼ C carob powder

¼ C raspberry conserves,
   fruit sweetened

3 T almond mylk or soy mylk

3 T coconut oil

2 T agave nectar or other sweetener

In a small sauce pan, put all the ingredients and whisk together. Heat to just before a simmer. Serve hot over dairy-less ice cream, frozen fruit ice cream (p. 181– Champion Juicer), frozen slices of fruit and cakes.

Vegan Chocolate Frosting
1 cake's worth

24 oz silken tofu

4 T maple syrup

1 tsp vanilla

1 10 oz pkg. Sunspire semi-sweet
   choc. chips

In a food processor combine tofu, maple syrup and vanilla until smooth.

In a double boiler or pan on low heat, melt chocolate chips completely. Add to processor and mix.

> *As the fog of amnesia disperses, there is a transformation in your relationship to other species, and in your commitment to them.*
>
> *Thinking Like a Mountain—Towards a Council of All Beings*
> by John Seed, Joanna Macy, Arne Naess & Pat Fleming
>
> www.Joannamacy.net

Very Berry Fruit Sauce

Makes 3 cups

1 C unfiltered apple juice
1 C maple syrup
1 T arrowroot powder
1 cinnamon stick
1 C fresh or frozen blackberries, blueberries, raspberries or other berries

In a medium sauce pan, put all the ingredients, except the berries, and stir until the arrowroot powder is dissolved. Bring to a simmer and simmer until it begins to thicken, 1 minute. Remove from heat and add the berries and stir.

Serve hot over pancakes or dessert crepes.

Zesty Lemon Frosting

Makes 1 cup

1 C firm tofu
½ C agave nectar
¼ C coconut oil, melted

¼ C fresh lemon juice
2 tsp finely grated lemon rind

In a blender, put all the ingredients, except the grated lemon rind, and blend until smooth and creamy. Stop the blender, add the grated lemon rind and pulse once to mix. Chilling for 10 minutes will help firm-up this frosting.

> *The good news is that we do not need a majority to shift the planetary mind toward peace; it may take just one percent of our population.*
>
> Gabriel Cousins, *Sevenfold Peace*

 # Pies

Chocolate Passion Pie

12 + servings

1 raw pie crust (p. 179)
2 cans coconut milk
3 T agar agar flakes
1 T cardamom
24 oz pkg. semi sweet
   chocolate chips
2 T maple syrup

Options:
Add 4 T crystallized ginger
or 1 C fresh raspberries into pie.

Bring coconut milk to a boil over medium high heat

Add agar and continue boiling for 5 minutes, stirring constantly with a whisk.

Add remaining ingredients and return to a bubbling simmer, while continuing to stir.

Remove from heat and pour into pie crust.

Let cool for a few minutes, then refrigerate for 3 or 4 hours or freeze for 1 hour and, then keep in fridge until time to serve.

Reputed to be the finest chocolate dessert ever.
Beware! This pie has been known to have surprisingly pleasurable effects!

Optional **Pumpkin Pie**, Blend 4 C pre-cooked sweet Kabocha squash, well with 1 can cooked coconut milk/agar mixture, ½ C cashews soaked 4 hours, ½ C agave nectar, 1-2 tsp pumpkin pie spice and 1 T finely grated ginger. Pour into pie crust and let cool in fridge.

> *There are forces at work in our culture that tell us we are separate from life. But there are forces at work in our hearts that are helping us to awaken, and take our place on this Earth in harmony with the other beings who draw breath from the same source as we do. We are not here to abuse and exploit other creatures. We are here to live and help live. Every meal is part of the journey.*
>
> John Robbins, *The Food Revolution*

Mango Mousse Dream Pie

8-12 servings

1 raw pie crust (p. 179)
1 can coconut milk
2.5 T agar agar flakes
1 T cardamom powder

½ C raw cashews or mac nuts
3 C mango chunks or similar fruit
   (mamay, banana, etc.)
¼ C coconut butter
½ C raw honey or agave nectar

Optional topping
½ C raw cashews or mac nuts blended with enough water to make a creamy consistency. Add 2 T raw coconut oil and 2 T agave nectar and 1 tsp nutmeg. Blend well. Add optional topping after about 20 minutes of congealing.

Prepare crust, except grind nuts less finely and place in pie dish, spreading evenly on bottom and sides without pressing.

Bring coconut milk and agar agar to a boil, add cardamom and lower to minimum heat to continue boiling for 5 minutes, stirring often with a wire whisk. Remove from heat.

In a glass blender, blend nuts with enough water to make creamy. Add coconut milk to blender with 2 C mango, coco butter, sweetener and blend well. Pour into crumbly crust. Place in freezer and allow to congeal (about 1–2 hours).

> *Some Christian mystics have called it the Christ within; Buddhists call it your Buddha nature; for Hindus it is Atman, the indwelling God. When you are in touch with that dimension within yourself—and being in touch with it is your natural state, not some miraculous achievement—all your actions and relationships will reflect the oneness with all life that you sense deep within. This is love.*
>
> Eckhart Tolle, *A New Earth*

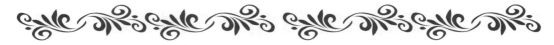

Raw Pina Colada Dream Pie
8–12 servings

½ C gogi berries
1 C walnuts or mac nuts
1 C coconut flakes
¼ C agave nectar
2 tsp cinnamon powder
opt: 2 T coconut oil
opt: 2 T cacao nibs

1 small ripe pineapple, cored, peeled
   and chopped
4 ripe bananas
1 C coconut flakes
¼-½ C raw coconut oil
¼ C raw honey
1 T cardamom powder

Finely chop gogis in a coffee grinder.
Rough chop nuts in food processor and
move to mixing bowl.
Add all crust ingredients to bowl and
mix well. Loosely place on the bottom of
a 8.5 x 11-inch glass baking dish.

Place rest of ingredients in food
processor and pulse to a creamy
consistency

Pour pineapple mixture into raw pie
crust and leave in freezer until well set,
(2-3 hours).

Raw Pie Crust
Makes 1 delicious crust

1 ½ C mac nuts, raw
1 ½ C coconut flakes, raw
½ C packed dates, pitted,
   soaked and chopped
1 T raw coconut oil
2 tsp cinnamon powder
½ tsp fine crystal salt

In a food processor: Process mac nuts to medium
fine consistency and remove. Whip coconut flakes
for 1 minute, then remove. Return all ingredients to
processor and mix thoroughly.
Form crust in the bottom and sides of a 9" glass pie
plate, firmly pressing into place.
Refrigerate while prepping fillings.

Endless Options include adding cacao nibs or ground gogi berries, substituting or
adding other dried fruits for some of the dates, and using other kinds of nuts.

Tropical Fruit Pie (Raw)
8 wonderful servings

1 large mango
1 C dried mango, soaked 1 hour in
 ¾ C water
1 C sliced bananas
1 C papaya chunks

Opt: 1 C raw cashews
 soaked 2 hours
4 soaked Medjal dates
½ C water
2 tsp cardamom powder

In a food processor, blend half of the fresh mango with soaked dried
mango and add half of the mixture to the bottom of the crust.
Add all the fruit, placing in an orderly, artistic fashion.
Pour the rest of the mango mixture over the top and gently mix in.

For an extra taste treat, blend cashews with the rest of the ingredients to a smooth
consistency and pour over the top of the pie. Freeze for 1 hour to set.
Remove from freezer and serve after 15 minutes.

Instead of dried mango, ½ C of soaked cashews blended with ½ cup of bananas or
peaches may be used for a binder with the fresh mango.

*The parade of worldly rulers, no matter what grand temples they may
have built, will be remembered only by the filth they have bequeathed to
their descendants.*

Anastasia's words from "The Space of Love" by Vladimir Megre,
translated by John Woodsworth. Ringing Cedars Press, 2005.

Raw Holy Cacao Pie by Grace
4-12 servings

Crust
⅔ C Medjal dates
⅓ C black figs (6)
1 C mac nuts
1 C walnuts
2 T cacao powder
½ C coconut flakes

Filling
1 C raw cashews
3-4 C water or gogi berry soak mylk
4 med. apple bananas
1 large ripe avocado
½ C or more raw cacao powder
⅓ to ½ C raw honey or agave nectar
2-3 T pure alcohol free vanilla extract

Add all ingredients to a food processor and pulse chop to a crunchy consistency.
Press into a glass pie dish and put in freezer to set.

Add cashew to a blender and pulse chop to a fine powder consistency.
Add water or soak mylk from 1 C gogis soaked in 3 C Awesome Sesame Mylk (p. 49) for 1-2 hours
Add rest of ingredients and blend to a creamy consistency. If needed, add a minimum amount more water as required for blending.
Pour filling into crust and freeze for a few hours.

Remove from freezer about 1 hour prior to serving your
Divinely delicious Cacao Pie.

and in **The End**
"The last shall be first and the first shall be last."
Christ

Recipe for a Fruitful Life

PRAYER OF ST. FRANCIS

Lord make me an instrument of Your peace.

Where there is hatred, let me sow love.

Where there is injury, pardon

And where there is doubting ...
let me ... bring Your faith.

And Lord, make me an instrument of Your peace.

And where there is despairing, let me bring Your hope.

Where there is darkness, Your light

And where there is sadness ...
let me … bring ...Your joy.

O Divine Master, grant that I might seek,
not so much to be consoled, as to console.

To be understood as to understand,
not so much to be loved, as to love another.

For it is in giving, that we now receive.

It is in pardoning, that we are now pardoned

And it is in dying ... that we... are now born again,

And Lord make me an instrument of Your peace.

Where there is Darkness let me ... bring ...Your Light

And lord make me an instrument of Your peace.

And where there is hatred ... let me ... bring ...Your love.

St Francis—the patron saint of harmlessness who embodied
this practice so wholly that wild creatures felt at ease in his presence.

"Mother's Love"

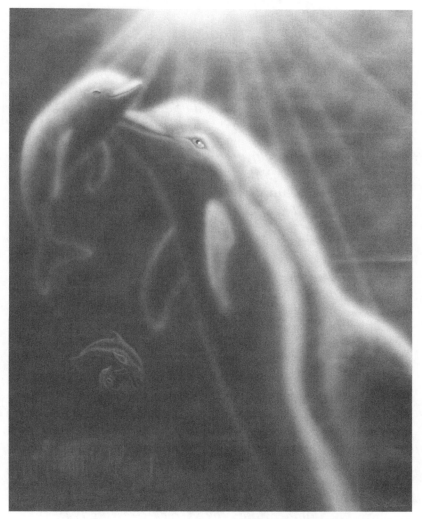

Daniel Holeman– Awakeningvisions.com

Saints and Sages say: "Divine Mother is hiding everywhere."

Nirvanananda

Vegan Cooking Sample Menus

"Rainbow Fusion Cuisine"

**Thai Coconut Lemongrass Kabocha Curry (143), Basmati Rice
Asian Tofu Vegetable Delight (127), Nirvana Sauce (94),
Green Papaya Carrot Salad (63), Mandala Salad (66), Miso Magic Dressing
(76), Tapioca Pudding (165), Lillikoi Passion Sauce (173)**

**Simply Delicious Tempeh (140), Italian Vegetables (120), Angel Hair Rice
Pasta/ Peaceful Pesto Sauce (95), Green Olive Tapenade (80),
Greek Salad (62), Sun-dried Tomato Balsamic Dressing (77),
Chocolate Passion Pie (177)**

**Krishna Cakes (137), Bliss Sauce (91),
Ayurvedic Indian Vegetables (113), Apricot Apple Chutney (79),
Spicy Indian Rice (141), Mandala Garden Salad (76),
Sweet and Sour Dressing (77), Prasad (151), Amma Chai (51)**

**Zucchini Love Boats (145), Walnut Sage Sauce (98),
Herb Roasted Potatoes (119), Tofu Sour Cream (83),
Tempeh Salad—main course style (70), Cole Slaw (66), Dill Tofu
Dressing (73), Apple Bake (160), Maple Whip (173)**

**Exotic Wild Rice Pilaf, Hot Thyme Sauce (93), Mock Chicken Tofu (139,
Baked Garnet Yams/ Cinnamon Coconut Butter Glaze (114),
Roasted Walnuts (82), Italian Dressing (75), Ginger Plum Cobbler (162)**

**Mama Mia Spanish Casserole (138) or Quinoa Black Bean
Enchiladas (140), Guacamole (87), Yellow Tomato Salsa (84),
Sunny Summer Salad (69), Greek Dressing (74),
Lemon Poppy Seed Cake (169), Zesty Lemon Frosting (176)**

Buddha Balls (129), Gombu sauce ((92),
Sushi Platter (142), Miso Soup (110), Cabbage Salad/Arame (59),
Raw Pina Colada (179)

Creamy Carrot Ginger Soup (99), Indian Tofu Vegetables/
Erin's Magic Sauce (92), Steamed Quinoa, Asian Salad (58),
Ginger Vanilla Chai Cacao Dreams (164)

Indian Vegetable Curry (134), Brown Basmati Rice
Indian Dahl (131), Mango Apple Chutney (81), Roasted Cashews (82),
Cucumber Raita (79), Carrot Raisin Salad (60),
Temple Bliss Balls (154), Indian Chai (52)

Forbidden Rice Medley /Tempeh Bacon (130), Secret Sauce (95),
Coconut Cinnamon Squash (114), Mandala Salad (66),
Lemon Tahini Dressing (75), Tropical Fruit Crumble (166),
Frozen Fruit Ice Cream (Champion Juicer 187), Cashew Cream (174)

Jia's Summer Rolls (121), Sweet Ginger Dipping Sauce (97),
Tempeh Thai Vegetable Salad (71), Green Beans Ginger (119),
Date Pineapple Muffins (158), Almond Mango Lassie (50)

Super Alkalinizing Juice (55), Raw Avocado Soup (108)
or Raw Super Soup (109), Sunny Almond Spread (89),
Mandala Garden Salad (66), Green Raw Goddess Dressing (74),
Raw Kale Salad (68), Holy Cacao Pie (181)

Lemon Lentil Soup (104), Curried Potato Fries (118),
Jaia's Waldorf Salad (63), Lemon Dill Beets and Greens (65),
Coconut Carrot Ginger Cookies (148), Mango Coconut Cream (173)

Marvelous Millet Soup (105), Corn Bread (117),
Zucchini Love Boats / Walnut Sage Sauce (145),
Kale Salad (64), Pineapple Cake (171), Cashew Cream (174)

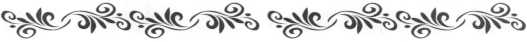

www.Kathleencarr.com

In the heart there is Unity. If you go below the surface, you will find this Unity between all human beings and all races, high and low, rich and poor. If you go deep enough, all will be seen as only vibrations of the One.

♥ Pathways to Joy, Swami Vivekenanda

Glossary of Ingredients & Terms

Agar Agar: A healthy gelatin replacement. 1 T thickens 1 C of liquid.

Almond Butter, Raw: A delicious, much healthier spread than peanut butter, consisting purely of raw almonds, ground into a creamy crunchy paste.

Arame: A mild tasting seaweed, excellent for condiments and salads. Prepare Arame by soaking in cold water for 20 minutes then draining.

Braggs Aminos: Similar to tamari and unfermented, with less salt. A delicious flavor enhancer though said to contain questionable structural components.

Buckwheat: A nutritious grain completely unrelated to wheat. Roasted buckwheat is called Kasha. Cooking ratio is 2 ½ C of water to 1 C of buckwheat. Bring water to boil, add grain, return to a boil, turn to low & cook for 15 minutes.

Brown Rice Syrup: A light-tasting sweetener about half the strength of honey, used frequently in Macrobiotic food preparation. Processed from fermented brown rice.

Champion Juicer: A favorite multi-purpose juicer that also homogenizes. A reliable juicer and the ideal machine for making frozen fruit ice creams, often using bananas as a base with other frozen fruits like mango, peaches and berries.

Chop = irregular sizes. Fine chop = the size of a pea. Dice = cubes of a uniform size. Mince = tiny uniform pieces.

Daikon: An oriental radish that is excellent steamed or grated raw in salads. It is best to remove the skin.

Dulse: An amazingly delicious lightly flavored sea weed that is excellent as a condiment on salads or lightly pan roasted to taste something like bacon.

Enzymes: Found in every part of the body and, like all catalysts, enzymes accelerate the rates of reactions that would proceed imperceptibly (or not at all) in the absence of the enzyme. Many people are Lactase enzyme deficient and unable to digest dairy products.

• **Digestive Enzymes**: are produced in the pancreas & saliva. Raw foods have their naturally occurring enzymes and do not diminish the body's storehouse. Protease = protein, Lipase = fat, Amylase = carbohydrate, Invertase = sugar, Cellulase = cellulose. Often supplements are used when digestion is weak.

• **Systemic enzymes**: such as Bromelein, Papain and Serapeptadase taken on an empty stomach are known to cleanse the blood, reduce inflammation, dissolve internal scar tissue, and have antiviral properties. Serapeptadase is the enzyme silkworms use to melt their cocoons. Studies have shown the benefits of this enzyme in reducing scar tissue in the body, enabling greater ease of blood flow and corresponding increased healing and vitality.

Flax Seeds: Nutritious source of omega 3 fatty acids. May also be pressed into oil, soaked and dehydrated for crackers, or ground and used as an egg re-placer (p. 18) or high fiber source. Blond seeds are a more nutritious variety.

Forbidden Rice: Newly available purple rice from China with an excellent flavor and texture. Called forbidden, as the color purple was reserved only for royalty in Chinese tradition.

GMO, Genetically Modified Organisms: This insidious technology is posing serious risks to our health, economy and agricultural heritage through cross pollination. Genetically engineered foods are banned in many countries.

Gomasio: Asian condiment made from roasting sesame seeds and sea salt.

Goji Berries: Highest antioxidant berry. Also called Tibetan wolf berries.

Guayakí Yerba Mate Company: A truly environmentally aware and active company distributing mate, a healthful and refreshing alternative to coffee that is grown in South American rainforests. Guayakí mate is produced as part of a mission to work directly with growers to deliver beneficial products that enhance personal health and well-being. Mate comes in many different blends, is full of antioxidants and minerals, and has a steady uplifting effect.

Hijiki: A seaweed very similar to Arame, but thicker and with a stronger taste. It is better when boiled for a few minutes before using in salads.

Hydrogenated: An unhealthy process that heats oils to very high temperatures in the presence of aluminum. Trans-fatty acids are produced which are structurally compromised and may lead to disease in the tissues of the body.

Jicama: A round vegetable with a light, crispy texture, and white flesh; nicknamed chop suey squash. It is excellent sliced in salads, used for dipping, or in stir-fries. The skin must be removed.

Kabocha: A pumpkin-like squash with a dense, sweet, deep orange interior. Excellent in soups, curries, pies, or baked whole on its own. Look for dark green, grayish to yellow skin and a high weight to size ratio.

Kanten: Also called aspic, is a jello-like dish made by boiling agar agar flakes in liquid, such as apple or other juices. (1 T flakes/1 C liquid boiled 5 minutes)

Kelp: A nutritious condiment and seasoning, this seaweed is most often sold in powder or flake form.

Kombu: A thick, leathery type of seaweed, most often used as an oriental soup stock base. Also reputed to increase digestibility of beans.

Living Foods: Raw, sprouted, dehydrated and fermented, enzyme-rich foods that have *not* been heated above 116° F. This is a light and pure diet, closest to nature, considered by many to have the most health and spiritual benefits.

Macrobiotics: A lifestyle and dietary practice espousing a universal way of health, happiness and longevity through a diet consisting chiefly of whole grains, vegetables and beans, popularized by Michio Kushi. He works with the understanding of what man is, what life is, and the order of the universe, then relates that order to biological, psychological, spiritual, and social applications starting with proper dietary practices and lifestyle principles.

Mycotoxins: Microbial fecal waste from bacteria, yeast, molds and fungus. Pleomorphic forms of microbes are created from negative environmental stresses. Mycotoxins tend to break down living tissue, acidify body systems and create a favorable environment for more pleomorphic organisms to grow. Foods with highest mycotoxin content are stored grains, flesh and dairy products (from animals eating mycotoxin rich stored grains), and processed foods.

Miso: A delicious, salty, fermented soy product, often mixed with other grains or beans and used as a soup base or stock. Add at the end, as cooking unpasturized miso destroys its nutritional properties. We use Westbrae or Miso Master, both unpasturized varieties, located in the refrigerated section. The lighter varieties are sweeter and less salty and more often used in dressings and dips.

Mylk Substitutes: There are a wide variety of soy, rice, almond, and other (what we term) "mylks" available. You can also make them yourself (see recipes in Beverage section). Look for organic milks without added oils, cane sugar, or vitamins. Our favorites are Imagine Rice Milk, Eden Soy Rice Blend, and Pacific Almond Vanilla or Hazelnut. Vita Soy's Creamy Original is also excellent. Homemade raw mylk is best!

Nut and Seed Cheeses and Pâtés: The use of soaked, sprouted, and or fermented (for cheese) nuts as a base for living food dips, sushi, etc. Nut soaking times vary depending on the nut: 12 hours for almonds, 2 hours for cashews, 6-12 hours for mac nuts, and 2 hours for sunflower seeds.

Nutritional Yeast: A nutritious and delicious plant-derived source (grown on molasses) of protein, B vitamins and minerals. Used to impart a cheesy or nut-like flavor and as an excellent condiment for salad.

Organic: Foods grown with care for the Earth through practices that maintain soil fertility and balance without the use of synthetic fertilizers and pesticides. These maximum nutritional value foods are free of artificial preservatives, coloring, hormones, chemicals, antibiotics, additives or irradiation resulting in far superior flavor and health giving properties. (p. 1, Organic Farming)

Probiotics: (for life) Beneficial strains of bacteria that help digestion assimilation, immune system function and vitamin synthesis in the body. Stress, antibiotics, caffeine and prescription medicine can drastically reduce populations of probiotics resulting in numerous repercussions including chronic fatigue, candida albicans proliferation and parasite increase.

Quinoa (pronounced "keen wah"): An ancient grain from the Incan culture, high in amino acids, alkalinizing to the body and known as the queen of grains. It has a natural pyrethrum-like coating that is removed by thoroughly rinsing & washing a few times. Use 1¾ part water to 1 part grain. When water boils, add quinoa, return to boil, cover and turn to low. Cook for 20 minutes. Excellent combined with a one-to-one mixture of forbidden rice or white Basmati rice.

Rapadura: A specially processed sugar cane product with the same sweetness as sugar, yet with a great flavor and the highest amount of nutrition of any sweetener, including honey. Agave syrup is now becoming even more popular.

Sea Vegetables: Delicious, highly absorbable source of minerals and vitamins: Popular ones are Agar Agar, Arame, Dulse, Kombu, Kelp, Hijiki, Nori.

Soba Noodles: Japanese wheat-free buckwheat noodles.

Spelt: An ancient form of wheat with a smaller more water soluble molecule, making it more easily digestible to those having wheat and gluten allergies.

Sprouts: Seeds and nuts have enzyme inhibitors that prevent sprouting until conditions are right. By soaking and sprouting, this hard to digest inhibitor is removed. The burst of life from sprouting adds many beneficial properties to the food. For optimum life force, sprouts are best eaten raw.

Stevia: A naturally sweet sugar free herb that is made into a concentrated powder or liquid extract, with a high level of sweetening ability and balancing for the pancreas. It is non-caloric, and used as a natural sweetener and flavor enhancer for centuries. Stevia is a much wiser choice than aspartame which was developed by Germany during WWII for brainwashing purposes.

Sucanat: Evaporated sugar cane juice in granulated form. It has about the same sweetness as sugar, but with much more nutrition and flavor. Sucanat is an abbreviation for "Sugar Cane Natural."

Super Foods: Unprocessed, natural foods that are very rich in vitamins, minerals and nutritional support:

♥ **Algae**: Spirulina, Chlorella, Blue Green Algae.

♥ **Bee pollen**: The male reproductive parts of flowers. High in nutrient content, minerals, protein and healthy fats, it is a high energy, rapidly absorbed food.

♥ **Cereal Grasses**: Wheat, barley, alfalfa kamut grass juice. Algae & grass juices are cleansing to the body and high in antioxidants, minerals, vitamins and enzymes. They are readily absorbable and have a high protein content.

♥ **Juices, freshly pressed**: Quality source of easily available, concentrated nutrition. Only the live juices are extracted, leaving out cellulose and roughage from the digestion process. With live enzymes and high vitamin concentration, juices are power-packed with life force and goodness. Juices are best taken separately from solid food and should be consumed within 10 minutes of juicing.

♥ **Nut mylks**: By sprouting seeds and nuts, enzyme inhibitors are removed and the spark of life is activated. These high protein, easily digestible, delicious mylks (different from cow or animal milk) are nutrient-dense foods.

♥ **Nutritional Yeast**: Great tasting source of B vitamins, 50% protein and a good balance of Amino Acids. A wonderful seasoning for foods and as a sauce ingredient. This yeast does not stimulate Candida as regular Baker's yeast does because it does not contain any live yeast cells.

♥ **Oils**: Flax, Borage, Hemp and Evening Primrose—highly absorbable sources of essential fatty acids, essential in many of the body systems, including inflammation regulation.

♥ Super Green Powders (See High Vibration Foods, p. 25.)

Tahini: A calcium-rich paste made from raw or roasted sesame seeds, traditionally used in hummus (p. 85) and as an outstanding sauce and dressing ingredient.

Tamari: A salty cultured soy product condiment. San J (brand name), gold label, is wheat-free.

Tempeh: A soy product that is produced through a fermentation process in a rice culture and is often more digestible than tofu. Boil or steam for 5 minutes before grilling or marinating to improve flavor, texture and digestibility.

Tofu: Derived from the curds of soybeans and comes in different densities. The silken is often used whipped in desserts and as a cream replacement. The firmer styles may all be flavored in an endless variety of ways, then grilled, baked, roasted, or added to

stir-fries. A good protein and isoflavone source, it is very important to use organic, as virtually all of the commercial soy crop is Genetically Modified.

Transition foods: A term relating to the transition from "the standard American diet" (SAD) to "wholesome health foods" and then to more "living" or raw foods.

Ume or Umeboshi vinegar (Eden brand recommended): Technically not a vinegar, it is a highly alkalinizing salty liquid from pickled plums, excellent in salads and dressings.

Vegan Diet: A diet consisting of food that is from non-animal sources (plant based). Many people believe that the choice of a vegan diet is one of our greatest ways to support health, morality, spirituality, ecological wellbeing and the end of world hunger. A vegan diet supports the practice of "Ahimsa" (Yogic principle and spiritual discipline where the least amount of harm or pain is caused by our thoughts, words or deeds). Many modern animal food production practices inflict a monstrous amount of harm and suffering on animals and use chemicals and antibiotics to keep them alive under abysmal conditions.

Vegenaise: A delicious tasting vegan mayonnaise used on its own or as a tangy base for dressings and dips. The grapefruit seed or organic varieties are best.

Vita mix: Considered the ultimate blender tool with super high speed, variable speed dial and a reverse setting. It has a large capacity and is strong and efficient. It is a wonderful support in the kitchen.

Wasabi: Spicy Japanese horseradish. Commercial paste varieties have artificial color. The powder is more healthful than the paste.

Wild Rice: Adds a delicious, nutty flavor to many dishes. Cooking proportions are 1 cup grain to 4 cups water with a 50-60 minute cooking time.

Xylitol: A processed sugar alcohol sourced from vegetables and found in the human body; reputed to prevent plaque, sinus infections and the common cold. It is used as, and tastes like, sugar without any glycemic elevation.

Approximately twenty vegans can live in the land required for one meat eater.

Gabriel Cousens, *Sevenfold Peace*

Art Work

Matisha- www.SongofHome.com

There is a Light that shines beyond all things on earth, beyond us all, the heavens, beyond the highest, the very highest of heavens. This is the light that shines in our heart.

The Upanishads, translated by Juan Mascaro

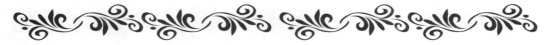

Francene Hart: Emissaries (p. 22), Healing the Heart (p. 37), Chakras (p. 45) & cover hands. Francine is an internationally recognized visionary artist. She utilizes the wisdom and symbolic imagery of Sacred Geometry, reverence for nature and interconnectedness to All That Is. Her work acts as a bridge between this reality and dimensions of healing and transformation. She is the creator of the Sacred Geometry Oracle Deck, ISBN 1-879181-73-8.www.francenehart.com

Cheryl Leigh Gama: graphic artist for the book, the cover etc.
Cheryl creates heart-song music, visionary art, & transformational mandalas, useful for attunement with the energetic pattern inherent in our bodies, and in all life, for meditation and stimulating creativity. She also paints tropical murals. Cheryl's artistic creativity may be viewed at www.ForeverVisions.com

Jean Love: (Mango Heaven, Cover)
Jean is a loving soul who deeply appreciates painting the beauty of the island, sharing her singing talents with friends, and growing spiritually. She is a delight and an inspiration to all who truly know her. She teaches by example.
Mango Heaven is inspired by the cycle of the changing seasons. As winter passes, winter visitors leave, including the Humpback whales that have frequented coastal bays (background), and mango season begins. At the end of mango season, in late fall, winter visitors begin to return again. Jean's art may be found at The Art Farm Capt Cook, Hawaii, or contact her at JeanKingsleLove@yahoo.com

Photographs (view artwork in color at, www.Veganinspiration.com)

Kathy Carr: Whale reentry (p. 186), The Refuge (p. ii) Infrared photography capturing the radiance of Pu'uhonua O Honaunau—The Place of Refuge, Honaunau, Hawaii. Kathy has a BFA in Photography, is a fine art photographer, author, teacher and consultant for Polaroid Company. Kathy spent many years as a photographer at The Findhorn Community and Esalen Institute. She has exhibited widely at galleries and museums, and has been published in numerous periodicals and books including, photography for *The Findhorn Garden, The Findhorn Family Cookbook* and *To Honor the Earth.* She currently resides in Hawaii where she conducts photography retreats at her tropical paradise vacation rental property. www.tropicalhideawayhawaii.com
To see more of Kathy's fine art, go to her web site, www.Kathleencarr.com

John Korpi: (Butterfly with Chrysalis (p. xxiv)
John studied advanced photography at the University of Colorado in the mid-seventies and has been a resident of Maui, Hawaii since 1984. Maui is where his passion for nature photography emerged. For more of John's art go to: www.fineartFoto.com

Matisha: Dolphin Bubblering (p. 193), Dolphin Matrix (p. 51)
Matisha is an international singer / song writer / poet / humorist, who presents uplifting, experiential events including: Ecstatic Group Song, Humor and Movement and Ecstasy Breathing. He leads unique Ocean Journeys, Land Journeys, and retreats and sacred site tours in Hawai'i and Mount Shasta, California. He is also an avid marine life photographer and world champion bubblering maker with many of his beautiful photos on his website: www.SongofHome.com

Rev. Sheoli Makara, M.A.: Twin Dolphins (p. 196)
Sheoli is a group facilitator for personal growth retreats and seminars as well as a Reiki Master and spiritual teacher. She founded "Awakening In Paradise Retreats" in 1996, as an inspirational and beautiful place for introspection, rest and adventure. Peruse her wonderful web site for ocean adventure stories and photos: www.AwakeningInParadise.com

Daniel Holeman: Om Shri Yantra (p. 36), Mother's Love (p. 183)
Artistic talent combined with a life-long exploration of consciousness and devotion to self-realization has given Daniel an ability to depict uplifting and sacred imagery. www.Awakenvisions.com

Tim Page: Buddha (Spirit of Tibet, p. 128)
Tim Page is a world famous war photographer, journalist and author who was wounded multiple times while photographing in war zones. He was extensively involved with the Vietnam Peace movement and many other efforts for peace: www.timpageimage.com

Back cover– pictures: Photographed at various retreats:
(OM) Mandala Salad (p. 66) and Passion (Chocolate Heart) Pie (p. 177) lovingly prepared by Grace. Sunny Almond Spread (middle picture) by Jia (p. 89)

Krishna and Cow in the Moonlight (p. 136) Artwork courtesy of The Bhaktivedanta Book Trust. www.krishna.com. Used with permission.

Contributors

Sheoli– www.Awakeninginparadise.com

When our eyes are opened and our hearts purified, the work of the same divine influence unfolding the same divinity in every human heart will become manifest; and then alone shall we be in a position to claim the brotherhood of man.

The Upanishads, translated by Juan Mascaro

www.EarthSave.com - John Robbins
Earth Save leads a global movement of people from all walks of life who are
taking concrete steps to promote healthy and life-sustaining food choices.
Earth Save supplies information, support and practical programs to those who have
learned that their food choices impact environmental and human health.
They support individuals in making food choices that promote health, reduce health care
costs, and provide greater independence from the medical system.
EarthSave International was founded in 1988 by celebrated author John Robbins as the
direct result of the overwhelming reader response to the 1987 publication *Diet for a
New America.* John continues to support the ongoing educational activities of EarthSave
International as Chairman Emeritus of its Board of Directors. His latest bestsellers
are *The Food Revolution* and *Healthy at 100.* More of Jia's wonderful recipes may be
found in John's book, *May All be Fed, Diet for a New World.* Visit John's site at www.
FoodRevolution.org

Joanna Macy
Joanna's web site opens doors to the new bodies of thought, time-tested spiritual
practices, and pioneering group methods that are powerful inspirations to understanding
and action. She shares these resources in service to the revolution of our time: the "Great
Turning" from the industrial growth society to a life-sustaining civilization: www.
Joannamacy.net

Kumu Keala Ching -Nä Wai Iwi Ola (NWIO) Foundation (Blessing p. iv)
Kumu Keala was led to found this organization to perpetuate the Hawaiian Culture and
practices through Hula protocol and ceremonies, the use and study of the Hawaiian
Language, and by embracing the stories of our Küpuna past, present and future. NWIO
is a multi-generational, community-based educational foundation (Native and Non-
Native), currently collaborating with organizations that focus on modeling and living the
Hawaiian culture, traditions and values. Through hands-on activities, NWIO applies the
knowledge shared by our Küpuna through the art of hula and chants. www.Naiwiola.com

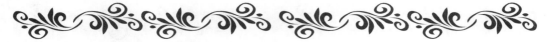

The Total Integration Institute (Foreword, p. xv) was founded and is directed by Diamond and River Jameson with thirty years of global experience as Expansion Guides, Visionaries, Integral Shamans and Wholistic Educators, in love with each other and with life, and committed to Whole Being Awakening and to the Total Integration of Being. They are committed to Sobriety, Impeccability, Love, and to the Awakening and Enlightenment of people, and the the world. They have traveled the world studying and integrating what works, letting go of what doesn't, and sharing what they know with others. Contact: www.Totalintegrationinstitute.com

Grace (p. 44) is a love-realized mystic, poet, healer and teacher whose loving presence and powerful healing energy has deeply touched the hearts of people all over the world. As an Essence Minister, she draws deeply from the wisdom of that ancient tradition, as well as from the life of Saint Francis of Assisi. She leads Healing and Meditation Retreats worldwide and lives on Mount Shasta, California: www.soulinvitation.com/grace

Nassim Haramein's lifelong research into the geometry of hyperspace has resulted in a comprehensive unification theory that has far-reaching implications in a variety of fields: www.TheResonanceProject.org

KAHEA The Hawaiian Environmental Alliance is a community-based organization working to improve the quality of life for Hawai'i's people and future generations through the revitalization and protection of Hawai'i's unique natural and cultural resources: www.kahea.com

Mata Vanessa Stone teaches and invokes the universal principles of Peace and Unity. Mata inspires all to live a devotional life steeped in remembrance of the Divine, Authentic Community, and Humanitarian Service. Mata offers the profound invitation to experience the Living Essence existing in the heart of all paths and traditions catalyzing an Authentic Spiritual Walk and actualizing a Deep and Holy life: www.AmalaFoundation.org

Recommended Reading

Berry, Linda, D.C., C.C.N. *Internal Cleansing: Rid Your Body of Toxins to Naturally Fight Heart Disease, Chronic Pain, Fatigue, PMS and Menopause Symptoms, Aging, Frequent Colds and Flu, and Food Allergies.* Revised second edition. New York: Three Rivers Press, 2001.

Cousens, Gabriel, M.D. & The Tree of Life Café Chefs. *Rainbow Green Live-Food Cuisine.* Berkeley, CA: North Atlantic Books, 2003.

Deluca, Dave (Ed.). *Pathways to Joy: The Master Vivekananda on The Four Yoga Paths to God.* Inner Ocean Publishing, 2003.

Dhiravamsa. *Turning to the Source: An Eastern View of Western Mind: Using Insight Meditation and Psychotherapy for Personal Growth, Health, and Wholeness.* Nevada City, CA: Blue Dolphin Publishing, 1990.

Goodall, Jane with Gary Mc Avoy and Gail Hudson. *Harvest for Hope" A Guide to Mindful Eating,* New York: Warner Wellness, 2005.

Hendricks, Gay, Ph.D., & Hendricks, Kathlyn, Ph.D. *Spirit Centered Relationships, Experiencing Greater Love and Harmony Through the Power of Presencing.* Carlsbad CA: Hay House, 2006.

Kolb, Janice Gray. *Compassion For All Creatures: An Inspirational Guide for Healing the Ostrich Syndrome.* Nevada City CA: Blue Dolphin Publishing, 1997.

Lerner, Michael. *The Left Hand of God: Taking Back our Country from the Religious Right.* San Francisco, CA: Harper San Francisco, 2006.

Lisle, D., Ph.D., & Goldhamer, Michael A., D.C. *The Pleasure Trap: Mastering the Hidden Force That Undermines Health and Happine*ss. Summertown, TN: Book Publishing Company, 2003.

Reinfeld, Mark, Rinaldi, B.O. & Murray, Jennifer. *The Complete Idiots Guide to Eating Raw.* New York: Penguin Books, due out in July, 2008.

Robbins, John. *The Food Revolution: How Your Diet Can Help Save Your Life and Our World.* York Beach, ME: Red Wheel/Weiser, 2001

Stone, Faith & Guidry, Rachel. *Yoga Kitchen: Vegetarian Recipes from the Shoshoni Yoga Retreat.* Summertown, TN: Book Publishing Company, 2004.

Tolle, Eckhart. *A New Earth: Awakening to Your Life's Purpose.* New York, NY: Penguin Group, 2006.

Williamson, Marianne. *The Healing of America.* New York, NY: Simon & Schuster, 1997.

Yogananda, Paramahansa. *God Talks With Arjuna, The Bhagavad Gita, Royal Science of God Realization: The Immortal Dialogue Between Soul and Spirit.* A new translation and commentary. Los Angeles, CA: Self Realization Fellowship, 2001.

Dreaming of a Vegan World

by Lorraine Asturino

Let's take a few minutes to dream we live in a vegetarian world. No, make that a vegan world.

Heart disease and strokes are uncommon, as are a host of other ailments linked to an animal food based diet. Health care costs have plummeted as a result of the overall improved health of the population.

Animal exploitation is a thing of the past. Cows, pigs, chickens, and turkeys are treated with respect and dignity. Wildlife formerly trapped or shot for sport now roam the woods without fear.

Millions of acres of land that had been used to grow grain for feeding livestock have been returned to forest, providing much-needed habitat for wildlife. Songbirds thrive, having recovered dramatically from their previously dwindling populations.

The cessation of human violence toward animals has had the effect of reducing human violence toward humans. The crime rate has dropped significantly as a result of the increased respect for life and war has become a nightmare of the past.

There is now enough food to feed every hungry mouth in the world because grain is going directly to people instead of being used to fatten livestock.

Waterways are much cleaner now that they are not being fouled from runoff from factory farms. The oceans, once depleted, are teeming with fish and other sea creatures.

Topsoil loss has been virtually halted, reducing the threat of desertification in many parts of the world.

Billions of taxpayer dollars are being saved because the Department of Agriculture no longer subsidizes the farm animal industry.

The burning of rainforests in Central and South America has slowed considerably, now that there is no longer a need to create grazing land for beef cattle. Because less rainforest is being destroyed, fewer plant, animal, and insect species are becoming extinct.

Less burning also results in less carbon dioxide being released into the atmosphere and contributing to global warming. The absence of over a billion head of cattle, releasing millions of tons of methane, means there is also less of the harmful greenhouse gas going into the atmosphere.

A vegan world would not be perfect, but it would be a much better world than the one we live in today. And … who may imagine what Great Mystery and our celestial family have to bestow when enough of us are truly walking in peace?

And in the end, the love you take is equal to the love you make.

Lennon and McCartney

Give Peace on Earth a Chance!